Scrapbooking
for the
TIME IMPAIRED

I AM

behind my boys

behind my husband

behind my family

behind my friends

behind the camera

behind schedule

behind in my housework

behind my scrap desk

behind in my work

That's me, always

Behind

Melaina Varble

Scrapbooking for the TIME IMPAIRED

Advice and Inspiration for the Too-Busy Scrapper

Kerry Arquette and Andrea Zocchi

cantata books   LARK BOOKS

Executive Editor
Kerry Arquette

Editor
Darlene D'Agostino

Art Director/Designer
Andrea Zocchi

Cover Design
Andrea Zocchi

Designer
Susha Roberts

Copy Editor
Dena Twinem

Created and produced
by Cantata Books Inc.

P.O. Box 740040
Arvada, CO 80006-0040

www.cantatabooks.com

Library of Congress Cataloging-in-Publication Data

Arquette, Kerry.
Scrapbooking for the time impaired: advice and inspiration for the too-busy
scrapper / Kerry Arquette and Andrea Zocchi.
    p.cm
ISBN 1-60059-003-9
1. Photographs—Conversation and restoration. 2. Photograph albums.
3.Scrapbooks. I. Zocchi, Andrea. II. Title
TR465.A75 2007
745.593—dc22

2006050412

10 9 8 7 6 5 4 3 2 1

First Edition

Published by Lark Books, A Division of
Sterling Publishing Co., Inc.
387 Park Avenue South, New York, N.Y. 10016

© 2007 Cantata Books Inc.

Distributed in Canada by Sterling Publishing, c/o Canadian Manda Group,
165 Dufferin Street, Toronto, Ontario, Canada M6K 3H6

Distributed in the United Kingdom by GMC Distribution Services,
Castle Place, 166 High Street, Lewes, East Sussex, England BN7 1XU

Distributed in Australia by Capricorn Link (Australia) Pty Ltd.,
P.O. Box 704, Windsor, NSW 2756 Australia

If you have questions or comments about this book, please contact:
Lark Books, 67 Broadway, Asheville, NC 28801. Tel: (828) 253-0467

Manufactured in China

For information about custom editions, special sales, premium and corporate
purchases, please contact Sterling Special Sales Department at 1-800-805-5489
or specialsales@sterlingpub.com.

Dedication

After school and during vacations the Cantata Books offices are flush with children. They race in to announce their intentions to go out—to the park, the pool or a friend's house. With sad puppy faces they plead that they are "starving to death" and need to order to-be-delivered food, or run to the corner store for a frosty picker-upper. (This inevitably happens within an hour of having been served lunch.) They comment on artwork, occasionally read over our shoulders and enjoy the hyper dynamics of a full-throttle publishing enterprise. They request copies of Cantata books to give as birthday presents to friends, for school show-and-tell and to give as gifts to favorite teachers. Our cell phones trill with calls from those children who are not actually in the office. These wonderfully distracting and loving kids infuse our offices and our lives with energy and enthusiasm.

Our children are our creative muses. We dedicate this book to them, to: Erin, Brittin, Ryan, Marco, Luca, David, Jessica, Samantha and Stephanie as well as the children of all our scrapbooking friends and readers. Without our kids, our lives would be incomplete.

Special thanks and an extra doggie treat to our supermodel puppy, Ray, and his family Celinde, Tim and most of all Cole.

106 I Can't Find the Right...the Right...WORDS!

...Introduction

In this hustle-bustle world, "down time" is as scarce as...as...(I don't have TIME to come up with a good analogy now. I'll think about it later)!

The problem is, of course, that without conscious effort, reorganization of priorities and some super-slick skills, "down time" is always just out of reach. And without those precious hours, it's impossible to transfer your scads of boxed photos into albums where they will be safe and beautifully displayed.

Scrapbooking for the Time Impaired is the busy scrapbooker's guide to getting productive. No more waiting for tomorrow when you can create scrapbook pages today! Inside this book you'll find terrific ideas for unleashing your creativity, creative solutions to scrapbooking when you're lacking supplies, and fun concepts for including your friends and family in your scrapbooking endeavors. There are shopping lists, scrapbooking-on-the-go information, speedy journaling ideas, time-management tips and oodles of inspirational fast-and-easy page ideas.

If you only have time to read one quick and easy scrapbooking book, this is the one to choose. It's recreational, educational and inspirational (so you'll be killing three "ALs" with one stone).

Have fun! Have at it!

the time is ripe

time heals all wounds

time is of the essence father time

[a stitch in time]

the sands of time   in the nick of time

Twenty-four hours round out a single day. And twenty-four, it sounds like a large enough number. Enough hours to get things done. But I am always wishing for more. More time, more time. Because there are always papers left piled on my desk at work, laundry heaped next to the washer, an empty refrigerator, dinners to be made, lunches to be packed, dogs to be walked, workouts to be done, bathrooms to be sanitized, carpets to be vacuumed, friends to be called, emails to be answered. And sleep, yes, even sleep to be had.

But sometimes, I skimp on sleep. Why?
I scrapbook.

I know what you're thinking. Scrapbooking? What for?
Let me tell you.

Because if I don't, life becomes a little more routine everyday; the days slide together into weeks and months, and suddenly whole years are missing. Because I am a shutterbug. Because I love color. Because I cannot imagine life without art. Because I love words. Because I need an outlet. Because I want to show my family that I love them. Because life is gloriously joyful and sometimes painfully sad. Because there are only twenty-four hours to sleep, eat, work, play. *Because each second is only a stitch in time, and I want to remember to live it.*

Mary MacAskill

Honey,
Guess what? Some guy at work was giving away puppies. SURPRISE! Look in the guest bedroom.
XXOO John

I feel as creative as a ROCK!

Have you ever had one of those days when you excitedly set aside time specifically to focus on your artwork, and then when you finally got chores out of the way and sat down to begin your project, you realized you were running on creative empty? The paper, the canvas, the cardstock stared back at you blankly and, try as you might, you simply couldn't figure out how to launch into productive mode?

Even professional artists can feel as creative as a stone upon occasion. The trick isn't avoiding the situation, but learning how to move beyond it. With a little help (the kind you'll find in this chapter!), you'll soon be racking up more creative days. So let your supplies take a little nap, and start reading.

What Is Creativity?

Opening up the mind to nonrational thinking

When you dream, your mind sprouts wings. Unconfined by the stimuli thrust upon it during the day—the sounds, sights, smells and demands required to perform tasks—it takes flight. Even while experts debate the impetus of dreams, you are swept away. You have sometimes frightening, but always exciting, battles. On other nights you meet people who impact you, stirring up emotions or opening your eyes to new concepts. And, ohhhhhh, the places you go!

Artists train themselves to travel inside their imaginations to places that resemble dreamlands. Their journeys begin with a desire to leave behind everyday realities and to grant themselves permission to do so. They calm their minds, open their hearts and allow their inner eye to formulate a vision. As it develops, artists pick up the tools of their craft and allow their vision to take physical shape.

Cammie Churdar

Creativity Abounds!

Creativity is not exclusive to artists. Mathematicians, scientists, doctors, engineers and others tap into the creative pools in their minds to better understand the world around them and solve problems. This artist found inspiration in Leonardo DaVinci's famous drawing, created as he studied the physical dynamics of man. The photo of the young boy works perfectly with the photocopied image.

Martha Crowther

The Creative Hearts of Puppies and Children

Before we grew into being "reasonable," our imaginations were the tail that wagged the dog. Mud puddles were our childhood clay labs; berries, our finger paints. From morning until night we allowed our dreams to take form in playacting and creating. We fell asleep exhausted but utterly content. To create, we need to get in touch with the unrestrained heart of our inner child.

Note to self
Puppies can make toys out of ANYTHING!
Remember to put away shoes, gloves, stuffed animals and plastic storage containers!

Creativity and Imagination

Creative people have shifted the weight from their left brain function—the side that is strongly developed in school and credited for success in reasoning, reading, writing and math—to the right side, the area believed to influence the arts, sports and insight. When we immerse ourselves in a creative outlet, we exercise the right side of the brain.

Marla Kress

Creative Affirmation

Positive thoughts have been found to strongly influence our success at any task, from healing our bodies to completing a job. Affirmations banish negative thoughts, which drag us down and make us our own worst enemy. Give your creativity a knee-up by dedicating several minutes a day to creative affirmations. Use one of ours, or create your own.

Make sure your homegrown affirmation…
1. uses the present or future tense
2. presents the thought in an affirmative manner
3. includes strong adjectives that speak to you emotionally
4. is worded so that success is the anticipated result

Examples:
1. I am a talented and creative scrapbook artist.
2. I will grow my artistic skills as I practice my craft.
3. I have many, many creative and exciting ideas for scrapbooking.
4. I will be proud of all my scrapbook pages and the effort I invested in creating them.

Lisa Turley

Creativity Boosters

When your creativity has flat-lined, it's time to change your lifestyle. Build these exercises into your day, and you'll find yourself rejuvenated:

Meditate Seat yourself in a comfortable, quiet place where you will not be bothered. Close your eyes. Begin to breathe slowly and deeply. Focus on the sound of your breathing. Allow your mind to wander. When your meditation is over, you will feel relaxed, energized and more ready to focus on your art.

Exercise Even moderate physical activity increases circulation, which floods the brain with fresh blood. An increased heart rate makes us more energetic and better able to move forward with tasks.

Take classes Step outside your own medium: You are a scrapbook artist first and foremost, but exploring other forms of art may help unleash creative concepts. Buy yourself a

hunk of clay, an assortment of oil paints, beads, knitting needles and yarn or supplies for another art form. Play!

Reflect Introspection can offer insight into the issues that are most important to you. If it is part of your beliefs, pray. This may lead you to scrapbook pages about important and very personal issues.

Read Pick up a book—ANY book. It will teach you new concepts that may ignite a creative flame within you.

Cleanse Eliminate toxins from your body and soul. Whatever your toxin, from anger to alcohol, it saps your creative power. Cleanse yourself and feel the newfound energy.

The Dreaded Block

Arrrrrgggggg. (That's the sound of an artist sitting down to write, paint or create a scrapbook page only to discover that no matter how hard she tries to focus her thoughts, open her inner eye, dream a little dream, she keeps coming up with nothing. Zilch. Nada. She has, in fact, been struck by the dreaded "block.")

If this scenario sounds and feels familiar (sorry), you have several choices. You can continue to force-feed your blank scrapbook page photos, journaling and embellishments. OR you can take a break and reassess the situation. Often, simply stepping away relieves the stress and allows you to breathe. (Breathing is good.) When you return to the craft table, focus on creating one solitary page. Just one. Chances are that once your creative juices are flowing again, that one page will generate a half dozen fresh layout ideas.

Shake Things Up

There are a million and one ways to construct any single scrapbook page layout. The eight variations shown here and on the next spread demonstrate how mixing things up and shifting them around results in unique page designs!

one

two

Marla Kress

Marla Kress

Go for the Extreme Image Use an enlarged photo, one so big it gobbles up half of your layout! Your engaging photo subject will draw attention and the simple design will save you time.

Layer Your Images Using multiple images on a page can cause some design headaches, but if you contain the support images within a corner of the focal image, it is as if you are designing with one photo.

three

Create Contrast in the Title This impactful title creates energy because of its layered effect. Pick two contrasting letter styles (here the artist mixed large block letters with a fun script style) and two contrasting colors for a title that says, "HEY! Look at ME!"

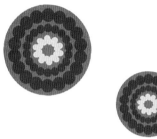

Marla Kress

Use Leading Lines A background composed of strong lines helps guide the eye toward the photo. The horizontal strips of patterned paper add energy and color to the fun-filled scrapbook page.

Marla Kress

Go Bold with Patterns This pattern-blocked background is a paper quilt of fun and vibrance. Group photos and journaling. Mat them on dark cardstock to distinguish them from the bouncy background.

Marla Kress

Simplify a Design Try limiting yourself to only four or five products for a clean and uncluttered design.

Marla Kress

Think Outside of the Title Block
Go ahead and get funky with that title. Run it on a curve, add shapes, mix up the fonts and letter cases. Don't limit yourself at all!

seven

eight

Marla Kress

Stencil It In Oversized letters make a definite impact on any layout. Have fun with stencils by combining them with patterns, personal handwriting or whimsical pen details.

Marla Kress

Finding Creative Inspiration
It's hiding in plain sight

It is said that mimicry is the most sincere form of flattery. In publishing, copying is associated with that wicked word "plagiarism" (not a good choice!), but inspiration and plagiarism are not synonymous. Being inspired by something=being excited and spurred on to make your own original, creative work. You may be inspired by colors, a shape, a technique, a phrase or some other element of a piece. Once inspired, you mold the element, mix it with other items, massage it and make it uniquely your own.

Let's get away together! John

Shannon Taylor

Honey...the Cruise is Fabulous!

There's nothing like a few down days on the high seas to inspire a woman! Those watery blue waves that buck and swirl and the heated reds of a sunset can really push your "I was born to be an artist" button. If possible, book a cabin on a cropping cruise trip. You and your fellow travelers will quickly be partying down with your baaaaad selves, doing the wave and sharing creative energy and ingenuity.

Be Prepared to be Brilliant

Think ahead, and you'll seldom find yourself without a plethora of great inspirational ideas. Keep a binder full of jump-start materials that you can turn to when your creative muse is mute. At first your binder may seen pathetically slender, but as time goes on, it will swell with treasures and you'll find yourself constantly growing your special binder library!

Heidi Schueller

Fill Your Creative Binder

Begin by filling your creative binder with the following:

- Clip or rip advertisements from your favorite magazines for great layout and type treatment ideas.
- Keep how-to articles from craft magazines that show super-cool techniques.
- Clip swatches of fabrics with interesting palettes, textures or patterns. Tuck them into pockets or simply glue or staple them to a piece of cardstock before putting them in your binder.
- Bind postcards or brochures featuring landscapes that lift your heart.
- Sketch and draw page concepts when they pop into your mind.
- Collect paint chips and store them in sleeves within your binder.
- Look for photographic images that evoke strong emotions.

Inspired by the Everyday

Wouldn't it be great if crop-cruise tickets or itineraries for romps to exotic foreign locales were included as part of our yearly budgets? Unfortunately, most of us are functioning on a bit more of a conservative shoestring (think, thread). As such, those mundane necessities—things like…like food and mortgages and health care…trump our travel plans. So where is an ardent scrapbooker supposed to go for inspiration? Why, just outside her front door!

Just Outside Inspiration

The front porch and all that lies immediately beyond are as familiar to us as our loved ones. Allow the lacy curtains that frame the windows, the flowers bursting into blossoms, the colors of painted steps and porch benches to inspire your scrapbook page.

Debbie Hodge

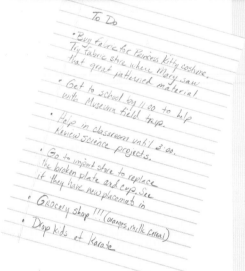

What REALLY Smart People Have Said About Enthusiasm…

"Nothing great was ever achieved without enthusiasm."
- Ralph Waldo Emerson

"A man can succeed at almost anything for which he has unlimited enthusiasm." - Charles Schwab

"Enthusiasm is that secret and harmonious spirit which hovers over the production of genius." - Isaac Disraeli

"A mediocre idea that generates enthusiasm will go farther than a great idea that inspires no one." - Mary Kay Ash

"The world belongs to the enthusiastic." - Ralph Waldo Emerson

Around the House Inspiration

Your own home can provide wonderful ideas for scrapbook pages. Draw inspiration from your children, family members and their favorite pastimes. Toys, drawings, books, even a beloved stuffed animal can become the subject of a meaningful photograph and a great scrapbook page.

Linda Garrity

Block Buster

Inspiration can strike at the most inconvenient time. High-tech and low-tech tools may help you remember those inspiring moments. Use your camera phone to record inspiring color combinations and patterns around you. Use your answering machine to leave a message to yourself about a creative idea. Tuck a small notepad in your a purse for jotting down those little lightning strikes of inspiration.

A Grocery Store Flier

A grocery store "Buy One, Get One Free" flier made this artist smile. The phrase seemed so appropriate when applied to her animal-loving daughter, who is smart enough to understand that if you buy the "mom" animal, future babies are yours as a bonus!

Maria Gallardo-Williams

Finding Inspiration at the...Grocery Store

Fruit displays Find wonderful color combinations among the fruits and vegetables of your grocery store.

Product aisle-by-aisle directory This big, bullet-pointed list would translate well into a journaling concept.

Product packaging Manufacturers pay graphic designers a lot of money to create packaging that attracts attention. Look for fun color combinations, bold and elegant fonts as well as page-layout inspiration.

Floral display Again, a great place to find color combinations but also textures and ideas for embellishment groupings.

Receipts This memorabilia helps create price-comparison pages (A loaf of bread used to cost__and now it costs__). They also are fun embellishments for day-in-the-life pages.

Makeup aisle Definitely the place to go when seeking complementary color combinations. Also, check out the applicators—they are great for adding chalk and other colorants to pages.

Product Package Sensation

This artist found inspiration in the package design of a cold medication. The lines of the package inspired the graceful sweeping lines of the paper framing the child's captivating face. Concise stitching, a floral embellishment, tiny ribbons and a large monogrammed letter take the layout from terrific to outstanding.

Miranda Ferski

Schoolroom ABCs

A schoolroom poster noting the laws of physics translated into an awesome page idea for this mom/artist. The journaling is nothing short of inspired, and the cheery page design carries the boy's glee in his newfound and frequently applied knowledge of science.

Maria Gallardo-Williams

Finding Inspiration in the...Classroom

Mini masterpieces Illustrate your pages and create accents and page backgrounds with your children's artwork.

Crayons and finger paints Whisk yourself back in time by decorating a page background with these fun supplies.

Gold star Give yourself an A+ by using these coveted stickers on school-themed pages.

Tablet paper Your little writer's wide-lined paper will make extra-spiffy journaling blocks.

toothless grin

No, I'm not ready! His first tooth is gone now. This is a sure sign. He's growing up! I ♥ this boy. Each childhood milestone like this one is leading him away from me. No, I'm really not ready!

sweet Robby ♥ 2003

Shannon Taylor

A Karate Studio Logo

The powerful swoosh shape from a logo found in her son's karate studio inspired this artist to create her own swoosh frame for her child's photo. The swoosh captures a playful and informal mood that is perfect for this cutie's pictures.

Logo courtesy of Japan Karate

Finding Inspiration in...Sports

Logos and emblems Re-create with paper punches, stamps and pens to use as embellishments.

Awards Show pride in your child's progress and achievement by using ribbon to mimic karate belts or the actual ribbons that have been awarded. Photograph trophies and plaques and include the images on your pages.

Inspirational quotes Look online for appropriate sayings that can be used as page titles or journaling.

Found objects Use shoelaces, trading cards, schedules and more to decorate your pages.

Shelly Boyd

Nature's Wonders

Take a walk to your local park. Take a picnic in the country or embark on a cross-country drive. You are sure to find wonders galore that will translate into scrapbook art. All the colors of the rainbow come together on this dreamy page featuring a photo of Mother Nature's own swipe of a paintbrush. The rainbow palette carries the entire design, and terrific photos of kids doing a puddle dance add energy.

Finding Inspiration in... Nature

Seed packets These make great envelopes for journaling strips. Or trim them into blocks and use them to paper-piece a background.

Seeds Create funky flower embellishments by gluing together interesting seeds to form petals and stems. Or encase them inside a shaker box.

Textures Let Mother Nature's lovely patterns and textures inspire page designs.

Botanicals Grass, tree bark, leaves, pressed flowers—all of these delicacies can be used as page accents.

Sonya Shaw

Spiky Inspiration

The leaves of a spiky plant inspired this artist, who used the pointed shape to create the terrific embellishment at the lower right portion of the page. The uniquely shaped four-sided accents (one holds the fronds) across the lower portion of the page are inspired by details on a terra-cotta pot. The fiery red of this adorable boy's hair is so astounding and appealing that it dictates the page palette.

Fabulous Fabric Store Finds

Whether you are making a Princess Kitty costume for Halloween, a quilt for a baby gift or an outfit for yourself, a stop by the local fabric store can offer a bin-full of exciting scrapbook inspiration. Check out the fabrics, of course, but don't miss a chance to browse the aisles filled with frips, frills and fasteners.

Block Buster

Does sewing scare you? Fast and easy alternatives to needle and thread include adhesive, staples, iron-on adhesives for fabric, brads, eyelets and rub-ons or pen details that look like fancy stitches.

Shelly Boyd

Gingham Fabric and Pipe Cleaners

The photo of this soft and squishy lamb being cuddled by an equally soft and cuddly girl is scrapbooked on a page inspired by traditional blue gingham fabric. The fabric is wrapped around cardstock pieces to create original photo corners. Pipe cleaners are molded into furry hearts and mounted over coordinating pieces of heart-shaped patterned papers.

Finding Inspiration at the...Fabric Store

Colorful fasteners Embellish pages with buttons, buckles, brads, rivets and snaps.

Zippers Use them as borders between two portions of the page or open the zipper and mount journaling or mementos between the rows of teeth.

Fabric Stretch fabric across chipboard or sturdy cardstock. Or quilt together pieces to form an unusual background.

Fiber Knit or crochet photo mats or use fibers to create borders and embellishments.

Lace and rickrack Weave lace and rickrack for mats and borders or lace it through eyelets and tie it in a bow.

Colorants Use fabric dye to paint or rub color on paper page elements. Use fabric paint to change the color of cardstock or paper embellishment forms.

Appliqués Seek out patches, rhinestones and iron-ons to match your theme.

Techniques Warm pages up with simple crisscross stitches or machine-stitch paper blocks together for a quilted look.

Felt and Thread

This little cutie loves sharing sugar smooches. Photos of her in the act are scrapbooked on this homey page. The warm and fuzzy heart shape is cut from peachy felt and stitched to the background paper. Straight pins embellish the layout and help secure the journaling block.

Alecia Ackerman Grimm

Awesome Art-Museum Concepts

Whether you enjoy modern or more traditional art, you're sure to find inspiration at your local museum or gallery. The shapes, colors and styles of art will shift the way you look at your own craft and open your eyes again to the fact that there is room in this world for all types of expression.

Last year, she almost quit ballet. Thankfully, she chose to stick with it. Now Caroline can continue to soar across the stage like a bird in flight, with reached high & feet off the ground. -2006

Shannon Taylor

Creative Family Crest

A boldly colored, romantic family crest inspired this artist. She cut a decorative shape from patterned paper to capture the feeling of the crest design and allowed it to overlap the photo of the young dancer.

Finding Inspiration at the...Museum

Brush strokes Identify the quality of the brush strokes in your favorite paints and mimic the texture. For example, allow a Monet painting to inspire a collage background created from mulberry paper.

Color combinations Abstract art often relies heavily on color theory. Look for bold and subtle combinations to bring into your own artwork.

Light How is light reflected in a painting? Look for interesting light angles to inspire new photographic adventures.

Line quality Dramatic paintings and sculptures have a discernible line quality. Some are soft and understated while others are bold and hard. Study how the artists used line and shape.

Frames Most of the paintings in a museum are framed. Get lost in the ornate details, distressed textures and rich golds of the frames, and dream of re-creating the look for your pages.

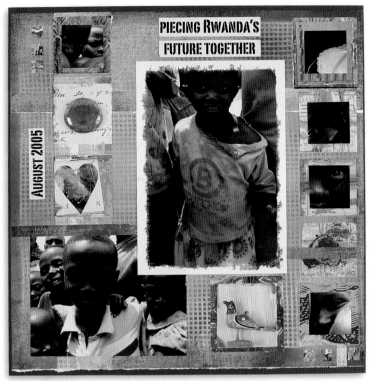

Sarah Fishburn

Make It Mosaic

A stunning floor created from pieced tiles serves as inspiration for this page. Not only does the powerful layout title draw on the concept of "piecing," the page showcases beautifully created photo and patterned paper titles.

Stained-Glass Sensation

Photos are repeated, cropped and pieced together beneath a delicate webbing of paper strips on this stunning layout, inspired by a stained-glass window. The shiny background paper with delicate scrollwork supports the theme.

Sarah Fishburn

Eye-Opening Import-Store Concepts

It is a treat to set aside 30 minutes to dip into a local import store. As soon as you step through the doors you are bathed in exotic smells, sounds and sights from other countries. Exciting. Intoxicating. These stores carry products seldom seen (around these parts) In colors and styles that make you want to travel the world. Use the products to inspire your own scrapbook artwork.

in
awe

Sydney
August 2005

in awe of the beauty and the mystery.

Diana Hudson

Play With Air

Windows cut in this bin offer inspiration for a scrapbook page built on a delicate grid background. It is the play of light and dark that makes the background work so well. The blue shade captures the calm essence of the water seen in the photo.

Finding Inspiration at the...Import Store

Place mats Create layout backgrounds from woven pieces of straw.

Paper lanterns Cut lanterns and use the paper itself as a background for your layout.

Batik fabric Crumple tissue, smooth it out, and then use a stamp pad to apply a batik-like pattern to the raised portions.

Buttons and beads Embellish scrapbook pages with exotic beads.

Picture frames Use lightweight frames to showcase photos on your scrapbook layouts.

Exotic art Re-create painted or carved designs with stamps, freehand rendering or with punch art.

Discover Pattern Mixtures

A combination of patterns on the cover of this imported journal creates delight. Like the fabric-covered book, this scrapbook page mixes patterns with strong diagonal lines and the direction in which they are pieced together.

if only there was a pause button to make time slow down - if only for a little while. jorpan 2004

Diana Hudson

goodbye

HUG

The goodbye can take awhile. First, they hide. They're pretty good at hiding, too. Even after they're found, they won't give up their hiding spot easily. Jump ropes and handcuffs come in handy - if they're tied and handcuffed together, we can't separate them, right? As a last resort, they will stow away in the departing car, hoping that the parents who dare to separate them won't notice. It's hard when your best friend lives halfway across the country the goodbye can take awhile.

Sydney and Olivia
January 28, 2005

Diana Hudson

Clean Up With Style

A fun and funky imported napkin inspired this artist to create a page based on its unusual palette. The napkin pattern was carefully—very, very carefully—cut out and mounted on the cardstock background.

spirit

CHAPTER TWO

I don't have TIME to scrapbook!

Tick. Tick. Tick. Up at 6:00. Breakfasts to make. Lunches to make. Tick.

Kids to kiss and send off to school. A husband to kiss and send off to work.

A house to clean, then a career to pursue. A kickboxing class to attend (to

firm up those thighs), a yoga class to attend (to calm down that soul), a

book club to attend (to expand that mind). Homework to supervise. Dinner

to make and dishes to do. Tick. Tick. Tick. Husband: "Hey, Sweetie,

remember ME?" Tick. Nod. No time to talk.

Finding time to scrapbook these days may seem impossible.

Here is the good news: It isn't! You simply have to set your

scrapbooking priorities. Focus on a clean, clear layout concept,

get your creative gears in motion and put the world on hold.

It is time to attend to the important business of preserving those

moments that might otherwise rush by and be lost in the yesterdays.

Find dog-sitter for night of anniversary

Scrapbooking IS a Priority

Pack up all your cares and woe and unpack your cool tools

We are told as children that being selfish is an ugly trait and are tutored to recognize the needs and feelings of others. However, when we set aside our own needs in order to nurture those we love, we eventually find ourselves running on empty. In order to give to others, we must also give to ourselves. That means setting aside time to fill up our reserves by engaging in activities that make us, as women, happy and fulfilled. This may mean exercising, seeing friends, laughing with our partner, attending movies or plays and, certainly, pursuing our art.

If you suffer pangs of guilt at the idea of turning on the television or putting on a computer game and sitting your children down in front of it with a bowl of animal crackers, STOP! Studies show that certain programs actually benefit your kids. (Make that your new mantra as you head to your cropping table.) While your munchkins are enjoying their downtime, you have an important mission to fulfill. You are in charge of preserving information about your life and times. This is no small task. If you don't take and scrapbook those photos and journal about events, these experiences will be lost forever. So get started Ms. Historical Chronicler Extraordinaire!

Note to self Surprise John with anniversary dinner — wine, candles, willing wife in something slinky.

Wendy Chang

Procrastination IS a Problem

We procrastinate because, on some strange level, it seems to make our lives more pleasant. It allows us to put off a seemingly overwhelming or intimidating activity and pursue another task that immediately gratifies us. It's amazing how many "good" reasons we can dream up for avoiding the task: "I need more time to think about it," "I'll feel more rested tomorrow," "I'll have more time to do it right later this week." Sound familiar? Hmmmmm? Well, here's the bad news: Once you delay the task, it only feels more overwhelming. Truly accomplished procrastinators then develop even "better" reasons for avoidance. And so it goes until the task simply has to be done—on a tight deadline and in a messy manner. So you don't feel good (understatement) and vow never to procrastinate again…until the next time, anyway.

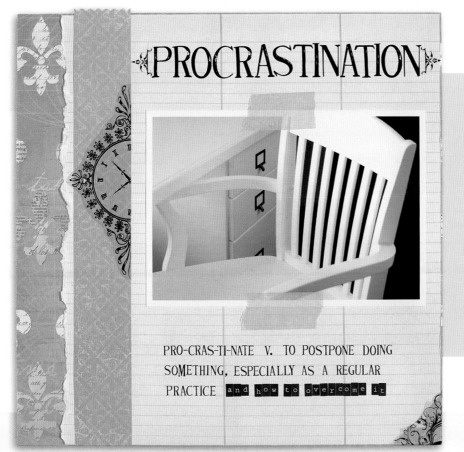

Diana Hudson

Block Buster

Are you the Queen of Procrastination? Get a scrapbooking buddy. Make sure your buddy is fun, organized and punctual. She will keep you on schedule and productive. It's always easier to work as a team.

Goal: Become More Efficient

Here is a step-by-step plan for making the most of the free time you do have.

1. Use a daily planner. First thing EVERY morning, check your planner for the day's activities. Keep task lists, important dates and phone numbers all in one centralized place.

2. Prioritize and delegate. Pick the tasks you alone must accomplish and rank them. Don't be afraid to allow others to help you accomplish the rest of the list.

3. Create a doable schedule. Next to each task, allocate a specific amount of time. If you are a person who needs breaks, build those into your schedule.

4. Mix business with pleasure. Include fun things you wish to accomplish (scrapbooking!), and don't feel guilty about taking time for something you deserve.

5. Multi-task. Listen to a book-on-tape while folding laundry or read a scrapbooking magazine while eating lunch.

Make Scrapbooking an Occasion

Everyone loves a good party, and that's exactly what a crop should be! When friends come together with a common love of scrapbooking and the intention to have a kick-up-your-heels good time, anything can happen. At most crops, that "anything" includes food, fun, information about new scrapbooking products and techniques and the encouragement to try them all. Throw your own crop party or help a friend have one at her place. Set out favorite scrapbooking magazines and books (yes, we hope this will be one of them!) and party down!

Wendy Gibson

Crop Themes

There are many types of crops, and all are equally fun. Here are a few of our favorites:

Crop swap Invite guests to bring supplies and gently used tools they no longer want. Set the goods on a table, label them and swap 'til you drop.

Slumber crop Get out the jammies! Keep the music pumping and the snacks coming, and most scrapbookers will scrap and chat until dawn.

Theme crop Will it be 1950s, with rock 'round-the-clock music, or a "fright night" theme with guests coming in costume? Decorations, food and games should support the theme. Keep prizes inexpensive and fun.

Technique crop With a little research, all croppers can bring an exciting new technique to share with other guests. Be prepared with any necessary products, tools and tips.

Scrapbooking On-the-Go

On your mark. Get set. Annnnnd you're off to Junior's soccer practice. Or perhaps you are heading out on a family vacation. No matter where you plan to end up, be sure to take along your scrapbooking supplies and make the most of your downtime.

Block Buster

Make your supplies do double duty. Adhere a self-healing mat to a binder cover. Now you have a work surface and a place to store embellishments and 8½x11″ paper.

what they say about idle hands?

I believe it

And that's why I always have a bag ready. Stuff I can do at soccer practice (while chatting with other parents) includes: going through photo indexes to select those I want to use, sketching and jotting down ideas, die-cutting titles, and cutting. I love cutting out details from patterned paper. After sitting in my chair for an hour it feels good to go home with a bit of headway made. May '06.

Debbie Hodge

Packing a Portable Scrapbooking Kit

You can't take it all with you, and, really, you don't need to. Plan ahead, and you'll have the tools and supplies you need to scrapbook on-the-go.

Create individual page kits Sandwich photos between sheets of photo-safe paper, and slip them into a sturdy envelope. Use small baggies to protect stickers and other paper embellishments. Put papers into a folder to keep them from bending.

Build an on-the-go tool kit A plastic container with a sturdy-seal top is the best option for transporting tools. Pack a good pair of straight-edged scissors, a corner rounder punch, a ruler, small paper cutter and craft knife. Put a small variety of adhesives in zip-lock baggies. A small cutting board can also serve as a work surface.

Splurge on a portable ink-jet printer To scrapbook on-the-go, purchase a mini printer (prints 4x6″ prints) that can plug in to your car cigarette lighter. Also, keep spare camera batteries, film and/or media cards handy.

Eliminate the Runaround
Taking advantage of the scrapbooking time you DO have (no excuses, please)

How many times have you heard a child say, "I can't practice piano because the dog ate my sheet music" or "I can't do my homework because the dog ate my notes" or "I can't walk the dog because he's not looking like he feels so good…"? As kids, we master the skill of excuses. But part of being an adult means putting those excuse-making habits to rest and making the most of the time you have to accomplish the things that are really important. Once you get started, you'll be glad you did.

You Have the Time; You DON'T Have the Supplies!

The definition of "super bummer" is to have the time to scrapbook but not the supplies. When faced with a bare scrapbook cupboard, some wanna-be crafters resign themselves to an evening on the couch with a pint of Triple Fudge Oatmeal Chocolate Chip Caramel Ribbon Delight ice cream. But truly tenacious scrapbookers rise to the challenge, finding solutions to the crises. With this book in hand, and some creative thinking, they ferret out materials they have hidden in closets and drawers around the house and devise ways to use them on their pages. (BTW, You'll find a scrapbook supply shopping list you can photocopy on page 127.)

Although crafting with makeshift supplies may require more creative effort, utterly unique creations will be the reward. Plus, the next morning, those who chose to walk the "gourmet ice cream" trail will be sluggish from their debauchery and bemoaning the hours they have to spend in the gym burning off the calories consumed. Truly creative scrapbookers—like YOU—will be happily organizing their completed albums.

Note to self
Create scrapbooking
Shopping list so I'm
Stocked with must-have
Supplies and tools just
in case I have a
chance to have some
fun.

I'm Outta Paper! What Should I Use?

Uh-oh. Wouldn't ya just know it? Just like that—from out of the blue—you've been given the time to scrapbook, and you simply don't have the patterned papers in stock to create the page you've been envisioning. What to do, oh what to do? First take a deep breath. Now shake yourself free of all your preconceptions about what a page should look like. It is said that necessity is the master of invention. So, get ready to master your fear and create the pages of your lifetime.

Hall of Fame – March 16, 2006

It was an ordinary day, just an ordinary day. A Thursday. When one of my dreams became reality. Derrick brought me red roses. And this is what he wrote: "You're the greatest! I knew you could do it! I can't believe how far you've come. I've watched you work endlessly, never settling for anything less than top quality! Your pages give so much life and they are so beautiful. As soon as people see them, they know that you are totally talented and you have got this scrapbooking thing going on. I am so proud of you. I'm your Biggest Fan! With all my love on this special day." Only he would understand how much this means to me. My sweet, sweet romantic husband.

TRUE romance

Mary MacAskill

Compose a "This-and-That" Background

When traditional materials simply aren't available, use what ya got! Pages from a book are glued down and painted to create this layout's background. Red cellophane paper overlays the book pages. Tinfoil photo corners and negative strips add to this terrific page!

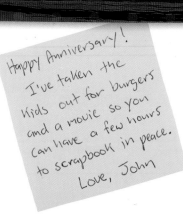

Happy Anniversary! I've taken the kids out for burgers and a movie so you can have a few hours to scrapbook in peace. Love, John

Block Buster

Guilt-Free Affirmations

- I am excited about setting aside time to scrapbook today.

- I will focus on the joy of my craft and be proud of my accomplishments.

- I am a good mother, wife, worker and scrapbooker.

- I will complete a scrapbook page today that records the activities of those I love the most.

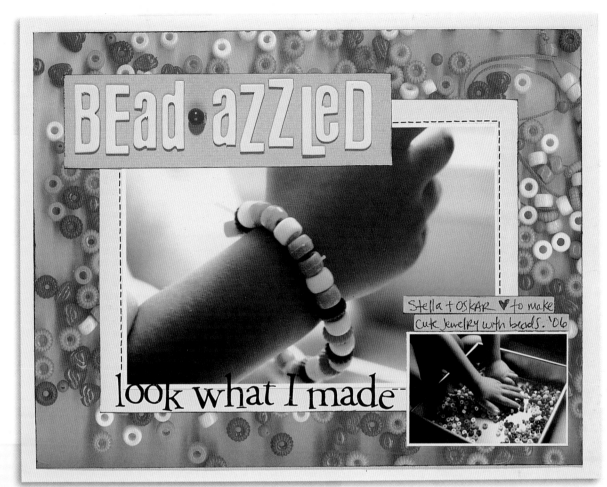

look what I made

Stella + Oskar ♥ to make cute jewelry with beads. '06

Alecia Ackerman Grimm

More Spiffy Things to Scan

- Jewelry and hair ornaments
- Spices and herbs
- Greeting cards, newspaper clippings, postcards
- Thread, yarn and embroidery floss
- Coasters
- Fabric, leather, vinyl
- Pieces of woven baskets
- Hands, feet, fingertips, hair, ears
- Fabric, blankets, sweaters, Dad's old flannel shirt
- Childhood artwork and modern-day masterpieces
- Ticket stubs, matchbooks and other mementos from romantic getaways

Scan Funky and Cool Stuff

A scanner can be a girl's best friend, as this terrific artist knows. In a pinch (the kind that was discussed on the previous page, so we won't bore you by going into it), collect cool objects from around the house and place them on your scanner on top of a transparency. The transparency will prevent scratches to the scanner's surface. Print the scanned image in a large format and use it as background paper for your scrapbook layout.

wicked **Smirk**

Miranda Ferski

Wrapping Paper to the Rescue

Most of us feel compelled to save wrapping paper. It's so pretty, how could we not? So when you find yourself out of scrapbooking patterned paper, open up your stash of wrapping paper. Remember that wrapping paper is not photo-safe, so be sure to treat it with de-acidification spray. Also, scrapbook with duplicate photos and consider matting your images on acid-free paper before mounting them on a wrapping-paper background.

Creative Brainstorming

If two heads are better than one, just think what five or six could accomplish! When you are feeling like you need a boost of creative energy, call up your buds for a brainstorming session and set out the brain food.

- Bring together a small group of friends who know and are comfortable with each other.

- Write a clear goal on a board where everyone can see it. Make your goal specific, for example: Name five seldom-scrapbooked topics; try five slightly intimidating but absolutely doable techniques; determine the best way to sensitively scrapbook a painful topic; concept five page layouts for a specific theme that can be created when you have no photos.

- State the question, then encourage others to free associate.

- Withhold criticism. At this point, all ideas are good ideas because they could generate another idea which could generate another idea...

- Postpone any decision. Allow ideas to flow. Twist concepts. Laugh. Turn concepts. Eat a chip or two. Keep things lively and fun.

- Take notes so you can revisit interesting ideas, should you wish. This will prevent you from stopping the creative momentum to explore concepts too deeply as they are offered.

- Revisit ideas to explore them more deeply. Ask probing questions such as: How many photos do you see on this layout? What kinds of colors would you use? How much journaling would be just right, and should it be first person or third person? Are there any interesting camera angles that would make the photos even better?

Tasteful Napkins

They come in lovely patterns and colors, just like patterned paper, and are inexpensive. Use napkins to create a scrapbook page background by adhering them to a sturdy piece of cardstock. Mix patterns for a patterned-block design. Or scan a napkin and print the image on photo-safe paper to use on your scrapbook layout.

Ah, summertime. We have so much fun together in the summer, and playing at Dow Gardens is one of your faves. The kids play area is so cool, and you love to sit through story time. You love watching the plants grow, and helping to take care of the gardens. I long for those lazy summer days, when we get to spend time together, especially after the long, cold Michigan winters. Here's to another lazy summer!

Kay Rogers

Definitions That Inspire

cre·a·tive (kr-tv) *adj* 1. Having the ability or power to create: Human beings are creative animals. 2. Productive; creating. 3. Characterized by originality and expressiveness; imaginative: creative writing.

flex·i·ble (flks-bl) *adj* Responsive to change; adaptable: a flexible schedule.

im·pro·vise (mpr-vz) *vti* 1. To invent, compose, or perform with little or no preparation. 2. To make or provide from available materials.

"go with the flow" *vt* (also, "go with the tide") Move along with the prevailing forces, accept the prevailing trend.

Nicholas - Asheboro, NC

Rough

See the hat?
It's backwards.

Not facing forwards,
not tilted to the
side. Backwards.

Backwards hat = Rough

Not cute, not
adorable

None of that sweet
baby stuff

Rough all the way,
big boy rough

Rough. Word.

April 2006

Maria Gallardo-Williams

Weave Together a Background

An enlarged photo that takes over the world can fill most of a layout. Of course the photo has to be super special—clean, clear and compelling. Scrapbook it on a piece of white cardstock that is covered with a woven mesh of colored cardstock strips. Add a bright title and journaling blocks to complete the page.

Hit Your Kids Up for Supplies

You've been a part of all those back-to-school shopping trips so you KNOW how cool your kids' school supplies really are. When you find yourself in a pinch for scrapbook papers, throw yourself on the mercy of your children. Notebook paper can serve as a really great background for a casual scrapbook page. You may also wish to scan and print the covers of those fantastic three-ring binders.

Dear Mrs. Welch,
Thank you for being such a great teacher this year. I'm looking forward to 4th grade but I'll miss you. So far you are my favorite teacher because you make learning so much fun

Have a great summer

Tylor B

smile   grow   learn

learn

SCIENCE

Tracy A. Weinzapfel Burgos

rASCAL

Cute KID

giggles

LOOK at me!

concessions and amusements

Samuel Cole

"Empty" Printer Ink Cartridges

How many times have you tossed those almost-empty ink cartridges aside and later discovered that you needed a colorant for your scrapbook art? Well, no longer, Lady. As this artist discovered, printer ink can be used to create rad "patterned" paper.

Create a Patterned Paper Background With Cardstock and...

Ink Rub an ink pad over the bottom of a shoe, along the stitching of a ball or the treads of a tire and "stamp" cardstock.

Paint Paint a nicely shaped leaf and press it against your cardstock. Repeat with varying colors and different shaped leaves.

Marbles Place a piece of paper in the bottom of a box. Squirt several colors of paint onto the paper. Drop in marbles and gently roll them around.

Crayons Tear two large pieces of waxed paper. Put broken pieces of crayons between them. Place several layers of old toweling on your ironing board. Set your "crayon sandwich" on the towels and cover with more toweling. Turn an old iron to medium heat and press against the waxed paper until the crayons are melted. Cool and use to scrapbook.

Stamps Use a single stamp design or a collection of different designs to create a patterned background.

Sketches or paint If you are comfortable with your drawing skills, paint or sketch an original background that works with your page theme.

Children's art Ask your child to finger-paint a special background using the colors of your page palette.

Veneer or Plexiglas Scrapbook directly on a thin piece of wood veneer or Plexiglas. Experiment by placing some images beneath the glass and others on top.

I've Got No Colorants! What Should I Use?

We learned to love colorants way back in kindergarten. Yeah, you know what we're talking about—finger paints! Remember how glorious it was to dip your fingers in those little pots and watch as a white sheet turned into a glorious page of smudgy color? Scrapbookers never outgrow their love of colorants and usually have a collection of inks and pens always at hand. But what do you do when you find yourself without? Get colorant creative.

A Spray of Colors

Anything that can add color to a layout can result in a terrific background with the proper execution. That's what this artist discovered when she reached into her paint cabinet and found three very different colorants. To create the red background, she masked certain areas on her cardstock and painted the exposed sections with stained-glass paints. Before those areas were dry, she moved the masking and sprayed with both whitewash and glitter spray. Paint power! That's what it's all about.

Samantha Walker

Samantha Walker

Make Up a Groomed Page

No matter how often you keep intending to throw out your outdated or almost-empty makeup containers, you never get around to it. Thank goodness! Eye shadow, blush, eye pencil and even lipstick can be used to colorize a scrapbook page when traditional colorants are not available.

A Kitchen Caper

When traditional colorants are nowhere in sight, it's time to open up your larder to find the walnut extract and food coloring! This very cool title was first stamped, using walnut extract as ink to create the shadows behind the title. The letters were then restamped using various colors of food coloring. What a yummy page!

Samantha Walker

Cool Colorants to Covet

Plan a colorant-seeking mission around your house to uncover the following:

Vanilla extract Looking for a gorgeous shade of brown? Grab the vanilla. Dilute with water for a softer shade, but feel free to sniff with reckless abandon.

Food coloring These work great when you need some primary colors in a pinch.

Fruits & veggies Add the zest of saturated color with the juices from robust pomegranates or blueberries. The beautiful textures of cut fruits and veggies as well as their rinds also make wonderful stamps.

Spices Fine, powdered spices such as cinnamon can be finger-dabbed and used to edge mats and title letters.

Coffee & tea For those lovely weathered and worn looks, reach for coffee and tea. Steep tea and use it as a dye or stain. Sprinkle coffee grinds onto paper, add a few drops of water and watch the color spread.

Crayons & finger paints Your child's art supplies will be an awesome arsenal of color.

Household paints Lurking in the garage are sure to be some buckets of old house paint or maybe some automotive touch-up paint.

Makeup Browse your own face paint for lipsticks, nail polish and face powders that can be used.

Sidewalk chalk Be reminded of how much fun these super-sized cylinders of chalk are to play with!

I'm Outta Embellishments! What Should I Use?

Embellishments are an addiction for many scrapbookers. And who can blame us? Stickers, those easy-to-use pieces of eye candy, come in incredibly handy for decorating photo mats, lending a spark of color to a somewhat bland page, adding balance to a design and covering up uh-oh's (pen splotches). Fibers are so fluffy and nubby you can't wait to touch them! And beads, baubles and metallics are pure bling. So what do you do if there are no embellishments available? Read on.

Samuel Cole

Hot Hardware Art

When the house junk drawers offer no embellishment inspiration, head to the garage. Those jars of nails, screws, washers, nuts and bolts can be used to create titles and add metal magnetism to your pages. They are perfect on pages that call for rustic distressing and also for male-themed layouts.

A new Leash on Life
There is only one Beat & Smartest dog in the
world, and he is ours.

Martha Crowther

Utility Drawer Finds

Open up any utility drawer and you're sure to find a treasure
trove of things you have been meaning to give away or store
away. Paperclips, rubber bands, trinkets and giveaways are
jumbled up with really nifty things like old dog collars and tags.
Collars that your puppy has outgrown, make great
embellishments for a pet page.

Must get organized!
- Clean out closets
- Get junk out of car
- Straighten out desk
- Old toys to Good Will
- Kitchen Pantry!

Katie Watson

It's All About the Bling

It is a rare woman whose jewelry box doesn't include unmatched pairs of earrings. We hold on to them because we are ABSOLUTELY SURE that someday the MIA piece will turn up. Nestled up against the solitary earring is a tangle of necklaces with missing links and broken clasps that we have every intention of getting fixed…someday. It's time to clear the clutter and use your mismatched pieces of jewelry to decorate your favorite scrapbook pages. The one above proves how pulled together your layout looks with a little dressing up.

Honey,
Susie says her new earrings are missing. Actually, just one is gone. And her pin that she made out of clay in art class..... The puppy again?

John

What REALLY Smart People Have Said About Self-Criticism...

"How shall we expect charity toward others, when we are uncharitable to ourselves?" - Sir Thomas Brown

"Self-criticism is an art not many are qualified to practice." - Joyce Carol Oates

"He is a man whom it is impossible to please, because he is never pleased with himself." - Johann Wolfgang von Goethe

"The most vigilant self-criticism of course is necessary, but the time comes when the artist must tell himself he is good or he will go under." - Gerald Moor

For his 10th birthday, I bought Joshua a knight from a collection he's been getting since he was 5. He opened his gift last and then his eyes started watering and I thought maybe he was disappointed. I started making apologies: *Maybe this is too young . . .* "No," he insisted. "I'm happy." "Are you crying?" "I'm just happy. I've wanted this one forever." Here he is a growing-up 10-year-old who still loves his knights. April 200_

much to admire

Debbie Hodge

Leftover This-and-That

Why, why, why do we insist on taking things like coasters home when we leave restaurants? And why do we insist on holding on to clothing tags when they have been cut off of new outfits? Maybe it is because a little voice in the very back of our brains says, "This could be useful someday." This page is proof. The smaller photo is mounted on a restaurant coaster, the fleur-de-lis is stamped on a clothing tag and the large decorative corner design is created using a chipboard frame as a stencil. All elements are painted to coordinate, which gives this page much to admire.

THE EVIDENCE: TEETHMARKS!

she

BITES

EVERYTHING!

HARD!

Miranda Ferski

Block Buster

If you aren't a hoarder by nature but love the idea of using "kept" objects on your scrapbook pages, get to know your local thrift stores. For almost nothing, you can pick up used clothing from which you can snip cool buttons, embroidered elements, leather straps, buckles, zippers and other embellishments.

Bubbly Bathtub Toys

Do you remember how good it felt to bite on something that was firm but slightly squishy and feel that pressure against your gums? (Experts swear that we can't remember anything prior to about the age of 3 or 4, so how can it be that so many of you are nodding along with me?) Well, this little cutie won't forget the sensation because her mom has captured the moment in a wonderful photo. The layout's title is created with bath alphabet letters similar to those she's munching.

I FOUND It in the...

Family room Coasters, long matchsticks, photocopied illustrations from old books, magazines to use for collage

Bedroom Old scarves to quilt together, forgotten-about belts, silk flowers, decorative purse snap, feathers from a boa, linens in need of repurposing

Bathroom Bobby pins and other hair clips, sponges for adding texture, makeup such as lipstick and eyeliners, gauze for light fabric-y texture, towels, bath toys

Kitchen Wine corks, bottle caps, coffee beans, seeds, dried beans, fruits and veggies, napkins

Label Art

Wrappers from products can be colorful and fun to use on pages. This layout, featuring a budding artist, is appropriately embellished with crayon wrappers. They supply just the right touch on a theme-driven layout.

Jodi Heinen

Maria Gallardo-Williams

Clothing Pretties

While the lengths of skirts and the shapes of sleeves may change from season to season, the one constant in fashion seems to be that designers enjoy embellishing their clothing. They add fanciful buttons and zippers, appliqués, leather flowers and straps. This page is decorated with flowers and leather snipped from the model's dress. (We assume she wasn't in it at the time!) The snipped pieces add dimension and color to the layout.

Kay Rogers

Homemade Stickers

Patterned paper can be the perfect option when you simply do not have the stickers you need to complete a page. Select patterns that work well with your background paper. Carefully cut out individual patterned paper elements (such as the flowers on this page). Combine them for major impact.

Honey,
The puppy didn't look well so I took him to the vet. He seems to have eaten some unusual things ... like scrapbooking paper or stickers?
John

Ashley Cantin

Digital-Download Images

Many Web sites offer free clip art you can download. Print the images and cut them out. Use your colored pens (or your child's colored crayons or pencils) to decorate the pieces before adhering them to your scrapbook page. Or, browse the Web until you find a colorful image that suits your needs (say, a photo of a field of flowers). Print the image and carefully cut out the flowers you most admire. Adhere them to your page in place of the elusive stickers you swore up and down you had.

Sticker Substitutes

Consider using these other items to replace stickers on your scrapbook page:

- Large decorative button
- Embroidered patch
- Punched and layered decorative shapes
- Cunningly cut pieces of fabric
- Broken piece of decorative pottery
- Small decorative tiles
- Colorized stamped image cut to shape

Note to self
Save empty egg cartons.
Use the recessed areas to
sort and save stickers
(once purchased!). Keep
cartons and scrapbooking
supplies away from dog.

The Magic of Mini Albums

Downsize your projects for ultimate efficiency

Hey, stop freaking out! We know that having time to create an entire album is an unaffordable luxury at times. If that's the case, pare down your project concept and create a mini album instead. Mini albums are the downsized version of the major album. The smaller format is naturally less intimidating, requires less of a time commitment and is a wonderfully inexpensive playground for creative experimentation. Purchase premade albums or create your own from paper, paper bags, old books and more. Mini albums make great homemade gifts.

Trudy Sigurdson

Keep It Creative

This album is deceptively simple. The inky edges, pattern mixes and well-placed accents lend a finished look to the project without being terribly time-consuming to execute. Once the artist determined the layout and color scheme, she chose a coordinating line of patterned papers from which to create the background. Since the papers came from a family of patterns, there was no guesswork or time spent finding papers that matched perfectly. Next, she grabbed a brown ink pad to add a hint of distressing to the album. She finished with easy accents—brads, ribbon and market tags.

Timesaving Tips for Mini Albums

Mini albums or not, these guidelines will streamline your production process.

- Use coordinating product lines for shopping ease, no-fail product decisions and consistency. Did you know that 8x8″ and 6x6″ products are readily available and these smaller papers will fit into your printer?

- Keep colors, style and design consistent.

- Focus on one topic.

- Keep accents flat, pick small accents that don't overpower.

- Pick only the BEST photos.

- Allow page count to hover around 12.

- Make journaling legible, paring it down if necessary.

Trudy Sigurdson

Keep It Simple

Don't feel compelled to reinvent the wheel with each page in a mini album. Each page of this album shows a similar layout design that consists of a photo, a short journaling block and an index tab. The colors are consistent. All of the photos are black-and-white, which unifies the pages. The same accents are used throughout, but are varied in placement.

Create a Mini Album

Album assembly is easy and breezy when you follow these simple steps.

1. Choose a single topic for your album and select only the best photos. Crop as needed and jot down journaling notes.

2. Pick or create a mini album and gather theme-appropriate products. Stick to two solid colors of paper and three patterns. Keep accents simple.

3. Sketch a basic page layout and begin assembling your album. Be sure that journaling will be legible when printed in a small font or size.

Becky Thackston

Love Mini Album

This tiny treasure imparts the story of a very deep, very big and somewhat unexpected love. The album cover is created from an old children's board book, which the artist cut apart, painted and reassembled. The complicated look of the album is very easy to re-create by mixing coordinating patterned papers, preprinted journaling stickers and rub-ons, fibers, flower accents and a hint of machine-stitching. The artist used a layered look throughout the album. Journaling is handwritten on pull-out journaling tags and includes journaling from her husband. To keep the album protected, the artist painted a wooden box, adding crackle medium to the top and sides.

Becky Thackston

Cathy Schellenberg

Favorites Mini Album

You can make yourself crazy if you begin to worry about what to include and what not to include in your mini album. Remember that the key word to this type of project is "mini" and that means that there is limited space for photos and journaling in your little book. So hit the high points and relax into the fun of creating the project. This tiny tag book is the perfect example of that approach. The artist casually selected her favorite things, bulleted the journaling, distressed the edges and kept the whole look and feel of the album comfortably casual.

Note to self:
Remember to take extra pictures of the puppy so they can be scrapbooked. Puppie is becoming "doggie."

Mini Album Themes

Select a topic you find interesting and dedicate an entire mini album to it.

- All about me
- Favorite recipes
- Hobbies
- Favorite sport/team
- Pets
- Best friend
- Advice

- Seasons
- Career
- A special occasion, such as a birthday or anniversary
- Club or organization
- Dreams
- Inspiration

- Tribute
- Favorite movies
- Weekend away
- Toys loved by your children
- Toys loved by you
- Where you grew up
- Your faith

Digital Mini Album

If you're at all computer savvy, consider creating a digital mini album for maximum time efficiency. Digital layout templates can be easily created (or purchased as part of a digital scrapbooking kit), making page creation almost effortless. This mini album relies on a single template plus a few variations. Digital scrapbooking makes journaling a snap and allows you to ultimate creative control over tasks such as photo cropping.

Sheila Doherty

Mini Album on Display

Mini albums come in all sorts of shapes and sizes. This one relies on a sophisticated letter organizer to house pages that can be easily removed in order to be enjoyed. The artist created the album as a wedding gift for her newlywed brother. Each page focuses on a detail of his wedding, including the cake, the wedding party and the pastor.

Keep It Together

Creative construction and bindings make mini albums unique and fun to build.

Unconventional mini albums Look around for funky things on which to build your unconventional mini album, such as a folded paper bag, board book, coupon book or a used book from a bookstore.

Tie it up Punch holes in the binding of your homemade album and tie it together with twill tape, ribbon or fiber. Or, enhance your prebound album with the same supplies.

Tape it Purchase book-binding tape in fun colors and wrap it around the binding to give your album a true bookish feel.

Loop it Punch holes in the spine of your album and secure pages with D-rings.

Shannon Taylor

CHAPTER THREE

I NEED to Get Started...but...but...but

Too many scrapbookers are intimidated by the pages they admire in their favorite scrapbook magazines and books. You know the ones we mean—the pages that light up, spin, open, close, sing and otherwise entertain viewers. Fearful of creating something so inferior that they would be embarrassed by their completed layout, they avoid scrapbooking altogether. Well, guess what? Terrific scrapbook pages don't have to be able to mow the lawn or defrost the refrigerator. They merely have to tell a story in a way that viewers find compelling. As such, sometimes the simplest scrapbook pages are the most effective.

Now for the bad news: While you can sometimes hide mistakes on chaotically busy layouts, cleaner pages require every element to be carefully thought out. So take time before you begin to scrapbook to envision your final page. Then grow your concept until it blooms into a piece of art. All you need is a creative jump-start.

Note to self:

- Excercise twice a week and stop worrying over losing those last 5 pounds!

- Clean out closets and give away unwanted scrapbook supplies.

- Find a way to finish 10 scrapbook pages without stressing.

"Simple" Is NOT a Dirty Word
(Just scrapbook)

The elegant arch of a country bridge; a whistled familiar melody; a single pearl—simple, but stunning. Many of the best scrapbook pages find beauty in simplicity. They rely on clean lines, balance and the strength of the photos for impact.

Because scrapbook supplies are so much fun, it is easy to feel compelled to use as many of the colorful, sparkly, shiny embellishments as possible on every layout. Not such a great habit (time-consuming and expensive). If Over Embellishments R You, reconsider. Designing a classy scrapbook page is much like designing the perfect outfit: A simple black dress and a good strand of pearls=classy. A loud patterned frock and loads of jewelry=tacky.

What REALLY Smart People Have Said About Fashion...

"Only great minds can afford a simple style." - Stendal

"Fashion is architecture: It is a matter of proportions."
- Coco Chanel

"Beauty of style and harmony and grace and good rhythm depend on simplicity." - Plato

Amy Jandrisevits

When to Say "Enough!"

How do you know when it is time to STOP adding elements to a scrapbook page? Ask yourself the following:

- Is the page balanced or does it "weigh" heavier in one corner? What can you remove or spread out to help lighten the load?

- Are the color choices effective or are there too many, preventing accent colors from popping off the page?

- Are the title and journaling emphasized, or do they seem to get lost among the chaos?

- Does the page rely on the title, photos and journaling to convey the story or the embellishments (hint: it should be the former!)?

- Is the sheer variety of embellishments stealing the show from the one embellishment that should not, under any circumstances, be overlooked?

Picture Perfect

Forty years from now when my grandchildren ask me who I was and how I lived my life, I will show them my photographs. And I will say, "No, I didn't live a perfect life, but my photos are perfect. They are proof of moments shared and memories made. They are proof of happy times, and some sad times too. They are proof of a life well-lived."

And I hope I will still have my photo wall. A place where I can display our favorite photos. Maybe then it will consist of photos of our children embracing the family dog or our grandchildren playing in the sand at the beach. Right now, our favorite photos hang above our bed in black and silver frames. And I wake every day to the memories of my life. Always changing, always growing. And I am excited for the future, for memories in the making.

[Journaled May 2006]

"A picture is a poem without words." – Konfucius

Mary MacAskill

Block Buster

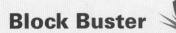

When designing a simple and elegant page, dress it in subtle colors (cardstock and supporting patterned papers). Use clean white type. Allow the photo to provide the layout with all the accent color necessary.

Clean and Uncluttered Creativity

Pages don't get much better than this one. It is defined by the fantastic photo, which features a simple display of framed and wall-mounted photographs. Black cardstock, white type, slender strips of gray striped paper and an elegant pewter frame complete the layout. It is simply perfect.

Take It Off, Take It ALL Off (at least the unnecessary parts)

Confident scrapbook artists aren't afraid to remove from their layouts elements that aren't contributing to the art. In this "disrobing" they actually expose the photo, the journaling and the structure of the page design. Without the extraneous elements, the words and images gain a sense of authority and impact.

From Good to Ba-Bam!

Patterned paper, a clock-hand embellishment and an oversized title add nothing to the good layout (left). Remove them, and the artist made substantial strides toward improving his scrapbook page. But the stroke of genius for this scrapbooker was the consolidation of his journaling. Some two dozen journaling strips and blocks litter the "before" layout, creating a sense of havoc. When the sentiments are corralled into a single journaling block (below), the text becomes much easier to read and the layout much easier to appreciate.

Samuel Cole

Product Without Purpose

A young girl this lovely needs no embellishing, and yet in the "overdone" page (on the right) the artist has marred the child's face with a bonnet of rub-on flowers. Six silk flowers, a ribbon and a page turn add more clutter to the layout. The page design is blocky, and the heavy journaling block in the lower left corner weighs the page down. When building the improved page (below) the artist created movement with the title, split the journaling into blocks that guide the eye across and down the page, staggered the photos and most of all—retired extraneous embellishments to the "some other layout" pile.

Maria Gallardo-Williams

Small Portions Are Good for You

Circles are fun. But half the number of circles can be just as much fun. Photos are wonderful. But half the photos can be just as wonderful. Stitching is good, but simple stitched buttons can be just as good as stitched papers. (You get the idea!) This artist got the idea as well. She proves it in her redesigned layout (below). She was much more selective in making choices about what to include and what to exclude from her design. The result is a layout that is fun and playful without overwhelming the eye. The title and journaling blocks are well-considered and used to strengthen the page design. The result is a page that breathes.

Wendy Gibson

Overselling Issues

Yes, a title is an important part of every scrapbook page design, but folks don't need to have it invade their personal space in order to get the point. The artist proves this to be true when redesigning the 2 "Happy Friends" page (left). The new and improved page (below) features a more delicate title treatment, which opens up the layout so that the terrific (truly terrific!) photo is easier to admire. The journaling is used to frame the photo, eliminating the need for clumsy, distracting photo corners. The final layout is 2 good to overlook.

Block Buster

When it comes to snappy photography, capturing the shots you want can make one say, "What the f-stop?!" Capturing an image that conveys movement requires a little camera knowledge. Either set your camera to manual mode and balance the light meter by adjusting the shutter speed, or set your camera to "shutter priority" (you set the shutter speed, the camera figures out the f-stop). Hold your camera extremely still (or use a tripod) and snap.

Shannon Taylor

Choose Great Photos
Develop a critical eye for evaluating photos

So…you've just picked up your developed film or reviewed the photos you snapped with your digital camera, and are amazed and delighted at the sheer number of usable photos you've scored. For a moment you're tempted to concoct a scrapbook page that uses ALL of your prints, but—like the clever crafter you are—you realize that using all those photos would be a challenge or even a disaster. Better to sort through the photos and settle on just one or two sublime images to feature on your layout. But selecting the photos to feature makes you feel strangely uncomfortable…almost disloyal to those that aren't likely to make it to your A-list. Time to take the "personal" out of the process and evaluate your photos with the eye of a professional photographer!

Watch Your Horizon
When composing a "dog-gone" cute photo it's easy to overlook what's going on in the background and end up with a horizon line that runs right through your subject. Placing your subject lower in the frame, as seen in the photo on the left, takes care of the problem.

Overexposed
When portions of your photo seem to be glowing and you are losing detail chances are your image is overexposed. If your camera has an "exposure compensation" feature, now is the time to learn how to use it.

Underexposed
This image lacks highlights, making it look dull, dark and "underexposed." If you are using a digital camera, the LCD display may be either brighter or darker than the way the image is actually being recorded. Try adjusting your display's brightness. If that's not possible, remember to compensate when taking future shots.

Location, Location, Location
This image has two big problems. Bad light (too dark) and a confusing background (same color as puppy). The solution is simple… MOVE! In the future spend time scouting your location before you start shooting. Doing so will save you time and disappointment.

love
DOG
FAITHFUL COMPANION
loyal
My puppy is the best
ball chaser, the best
rope tugger, the best
snuggler and
altogether the best
friend a boy
could have."
What more can a boy
ask for? Life doesnt
get any better than
this. We are so happy
to have our new
addition to our family
even if he is the BEST
and BIGGEST eater
the family.
Do not lose hold of your dreams or aspirations. For if you do, you may still exist but you have ceased to live.
- Henry David Thoreau
fetch
adore
arrf
Puppy dogtails
Doing a trick
A STOMACH WITH FOUR LEGS PUPPY-CHEWED
puppy
love
man's
BEST
FRIEND
to the

Martha Crowther

Scrapbook Only Winning Photos

This little pup and his young master is featured in a terrific photo on a super strong scrapbook page. The image is the very best photo of those taken during a single shoot (left). Clean, clear and full of personality, the picture is so powerful that it doesn't require support images or a heavily embellished layout.

Film is Cheap

Professional photographers take a "gazillion" images at every shoot. The reason is that a minor detail can make all the difference. Don't pose your subjects, wait, shoot, pose again. Instead, give them information and direction before you start shooting. Then fire away and offer "encouraging commentary" as you take shot after shot.

Great Pages With One Super-Duper, Very Cool Photo

When you're lucky enough to have a terrific photo to scrapbook, you are very nearly home free when it comes to designing a strong layout. A sterling photo can be enlarged, cropped, duplicated and manipulated to create layouts with very different looks and feels. Select that single photo carefully and let the topic of the image, the mood and the colors define the artwork you are creating.

Bravado NOT Needed Here

A small square-cropped photo on a single photo page can hold its own when balanced with other page elements. The image and the elements are mounted on a square of cardstock and popped up off of the background with foam adhesive, preventing the wide blue border from becoming boring. Journaling surrounds the mat.

Mary MacAskill

Mary MacAskill

Showcase Your Words

Make a page all about your journaling (for a change?). Use your single photo to balance the substantial journaling block. Add a playful title.

Share and Share Alike

This layout is a perfect balance between the journaling and the oversized, vertically cropped photo. The playful title strides the line between the two sides of the page, acting as a visual bridge to connect them.

Mary MacAskill

Front and Center

A photo mounted right in the middle of a background is going to draw immediate attention. But this obvious-mounting solution can also be stagnant and boring. This artist created a sense of movement and grace with the large oblong photo mat that extends beyond the image. The title, mounted across the lower section of the photo, further breaks up the boxy lines.

Mary MacAskill

Balance Layouts With Two Terrific Photos

Like a seesaw, two photos can be brought into perfect balance. Vary the sizes and shapes of your images to create a variety of layout designs. Use your title, journaling block and embellishments to add visual weight to areas of the layout that require it. Change fonts and embellishments to vary the look of two-photo pages.

Lisa Turley

Align Lower Photo Edges

The bottom edges of a horizontal and a vertical photo are aligned on this lovely scrapbook page. The first word of the title floats over the butterfly image, creating a sense of flight and balancing the two images. The second portion of the title stretches across the lower section of the page, joining a stitched ribbon and journaling strip to create a border. Silk flowers embellish the art.

Lighten Up and Spread Out

Spreading out the photos to opposite corners of this page opens up a large stretch of calm blue patterned paper for this multicolored title. The slender journaling strip slips under the butterfly photo, a blue photo corner embraces the photo of the girl. Decorative oversized brads add weight to portions of the layout that otherwise might seem empty.

Lisa Turley

Oversize Your Photo Mat

Two photos are brought together on a huge block of purple cardstock that serves as a joint photo mat for two images. The purple mat is mounted on a large block of stitched, purple-striped cardstock. Brads, ribbons and a delicate stamped butterfly design flit on the cardstock. A portion of the page title is created with rub-ons on the photo while the other half scrolls under the butterfly image.

Lisa Turley

Move Over Photos

When two photos are stacked on top of each other on the vertical edge of the paper, it leaves the other third free for a dramatic embellishment that includes a bright blue ribbon and several tiny three-dimensional butterfly embellishments. A stamped pattern separates images from the embellishment block.

Lisa Turley

Three Photos For Thrice the Fun

(Three fingers in appropriate "pledge" position): "We promise to show you four terrific pages using three terrific photos. These layouts can be used successfully again and again." And we are as good as our pledge. Take a look at the four fantastic layouts below! With these and your own photos, you'll be able to successfully scrapbook three-image layouts that are always fresh, simply by changing palettes, patterns and embellishments.

Debbie Hodge

No Help Needed

A large photo featuring two girls having altogether toooo much fun is supported by a vertical and a horizontal image. Over-lapping corners, the photos are grouped together in the center of the background paper. They are joined by a happy-go-lucky title, bookplate and tiny framed charm and chain. The stretch of bright, clean blue cardstock around the edges of the layout offers pools of visual calm.

Tiny-Photo Tag Team

A lacy stamped paisley adds a delicate touch to the top left corner of the focal photo on this lovely scrapbook page. Two supporting photos are mounted shoulder to shoulder on a spring green, ribbon-tied tag. The page title includes multimedia lettering and hand journaling.

Debbie Hodge

Mount Up and Head Out

Mounting two support photos on a bright purple chipboard frame gives this layout a successful shot of dimension. The purple embellishment in the top left corner and the buttons running down the right side of the layout contribute even more dimension. Flirty floral patterned paper, a piece of scalloped peach cardstock and a light green background complete the page.

Debbie Hodge

"Felt" Good Embellishments

The red felt, beaded paisley in the top right corner of this layout is just plain fun. The embellishment adds a round shape to this otherwise blocky page. The two supporting photos and the focal image are mounted on a piece of yellow cardstock. The journaling block extends the square shape into a rectangle. A casual title and flirty flower balance the artwork.

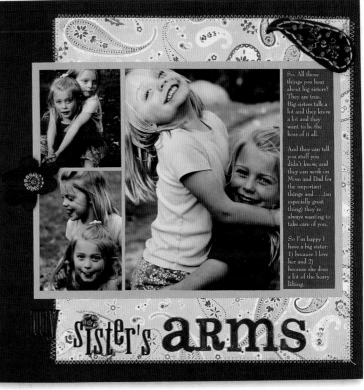

Debbie Hodge

Scrapbooking Four For Fun (We're Talkin' Photos!)

One big and three small? Two big and two small? Three big and one small? No matter how you visualize your layout, scrapbooking four photos allows creative flexibility without the fear of crowding. When scrapbooking with four photos, additional elements are kept to a minimum so as not to steal the thunder from the images.

First and Foremost

You are invited to begin your visual journey across this layout in the lower left corner, where the page title calls, "Look at me!" ("And while you're down in this region, take a look at this photo on my left.") The larger photo mounted at the middle of the page leads the eye toward the support images. A few strips and circles of colored papers and a journaling block dress up the art without upsetting the balance.

Group and Overlap

Two closely cropped photos act as bookends, embracing the smaller images between them in the center of this layout. Patterned papers, looking as worn as a boy's blue-jeaned knees, are playfully decorated with bright eyelet brads and nonchalantly tied fibers.

Samuel Cole

Samuel Cole

Block Buster

Don't be afraid to use an image shot from behind the model. Not only can tales be told from the model's body language, viewers find themselves being drawn into the scene as they wonder what is so compelling that the model is willing to turn his back to the camera to take a longer look.

Imagine

Three photos of equal size are mounted in a triangle on this well-balanced page. The fourth photo, while smaller, looks at the viewer with a direct and unflinching gaze from below. In a stroke of genius, the artist decoratively circled the eye of the model in the center photo with a cut paper "donut." Stamped words across the red cardstock at the top of the page and a journaling strip at the bottom supply all the information needed.

All He Can Be

This good-looking guy's better qualities are illuminated on this layout. Descriptive framed words, journaled strips and a tag provide information. Open up the envelope mounted at the lower right corner of the page, and even more journaling is available. A stitched ribbon adds a homey touch to this superb layout.

Samuel Cole

Samuel Cole

Great Layouts With Gobs and Oooodles of Photos

It is easy to mount more than a half dozen wonderful photos on a single scrapbook page. What ISN'T easy is to do so in an artful manner. There are many variables—the size of the photos, their shape, the amount of journaling needed, the typeface and the type of embellishments selected—and if misjudged, any of them can throw the layout into disorder. *(For a variety of great page templates see our never-fail templates on page 126.)*

Martha Crowther

It's Neither Here Nor There

The whimsical arrow cleverly directs viewers from the primary photo to the object of the boy's delight…ICE CREAM! Five wallet-sized support images put the ice-cream-eating afternoon into perspective. Only a short stretch of ribbon and a buckle are needed to add texture and shine to the page.

Look More Attractive, Thinner and Confident!

OK, so maybe that's an overstatement, but these page design tips will teach you how to dress your page in spectacular style.

What to wear with white White backgrounds can be intimidating, but what better way to show off this classic color than with clean, crisp stripes. Graphic prints also are a sharp choice for creating pages with edge. Use denim blue or even denim fabric for casual chic.

What to wear with pink Pink is the new black, but too much of it can make a page look as if it's been doused with Pepto-Bismol®. Pair pink with neutral shades (white, cream, chocolate, khaki and denim) to help ground it. Keep in mind that black and pink, while a classic combo, will look dated if the pink is too "hot." Experiment with the range of pinks—deep and saturated, light and flirty or the happy medium of cotton candy.

A Border of Boy Moments

Wallet-sized photos are stacked on this layout, forming a barrier between the two focal images and the text. The "eat here" arrow suggests that viewers can visually hop that border to get a closer look at the journaling. A stamped design opens up space in the upper right corner.

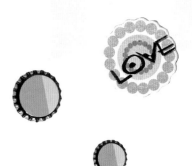

Martha Crowther

It's Up to You

Begin at the beginning (the focal image) and then make your own decision about which direction to move your eyes. You may choose to peruse the two images in the right corner or the four stacked images along the edge of the page. No matter—all choices circle the journaling block and lead back to home base.

Block Buster

When you want a series of perfect shots that tell a story, keep this mantra in mind: Film is CHEAP! So, take lots of photos, at least a roll for every shoot. What's not cheap? Your time and the developing costs required for a reshoot.

Martha Crowther

Streamline Your Scrapbooking

Eight logical steps to creating multiple pages at once

Cramming. Remember that doomed feeling the night before finals when you had not studied for that impending essay test? Scrapbooking should NEVER resurrect that anxiety-laden, coffee-fueled, hair-pulling, sanity-snapping feeling. Instead, be smart about your scrapbooking by looking at it as a task-driven activity. Become an assembly-line scrapbooker who groups tasks for better productivity.

Step 1: Get Organized!

Begin by deciding whether to sort photos by theme or chronologically. Take a weekend to sort your photos. Then, maintain your system with every new batch of pictures you take. If you use a film camera, organize and label your photos as soon as they are developed. If you take digital photos, download the images, delete rotten shots, name the keepers and create duplicate files for any photos that you wish to crop and edit.

Organize papers, embellishments, pens and colorants by theme and color. Store often-used supplies within easy reach of your work surface.

Step 2: Choose Photos

Select your favorite photos relating to the topic you plan to scrapbook. Determine the themes of the pages you will be working on and designate potential photos for each layout. For example, if you are scrapbooking Junior's birthday, divide the photos in to separate piles featuring guests, presents and birthday games. Decide which photos will be focal images and which are to be cropped or enlarged.

Timesavers

Think tasks Divvy up scrapbooking into a series of tasks that can be completed when time permits.

Plan Work on a batch of page ideas that fall under the same theme. Complete multiple pages at once.

Keep notes Carry a small notebook with you in which to jot ideas for pages (journaling, photo ops, layout designs).

Create page kits This is key when cropping on-the-go—assemble page kits with the photos, papers, accents, and layout and journaling ideas you plan to use. That way you can spend time socializing instead of planning and organizing.

Use what you have Save time (and money!) shopping by using what you have in your stash. Paw through it occasionally and challenge yourself to be creative.

Step 3: Write Journaling

Many scrapbookers save the journaling for last, but journaling early in the process helps you determine the voice and mood of your page. This makes the selection of a page design and appropriate products much easier. Allow your photos to help determine the energy and emotion you hope to capture with your artwork. Writing journaling for multiple pages at the same time ensures a consistent voice. Once journaling is completed you will have a much better idea of the amount of space to dedicate to text on your layout. Concept a title for each layout.

Step 4: Choose Papers

Select two to three solid colors of cardstock for page backgrounds, mats and other small accents such as photo corners. Next, choose two to three patterned papers to match. Don't feel that your paper palettes have to match the colors within your photos. Photos can always be manipulated to black-and-white if you have set your heart on using a particular series of papers.

Time Wasters

Disorganization A messy desk will clog your brain, preventing creative energy from flowing. A chaotic collection of supplies will cost you precious time as you seek out what you need.

Avoid distractions Try to scrapbook in a quiet environment where you know you will not be bothered. Make it clear to others that you should not be interrupted. Set a timer so children can keep track of "Mommy time" without asking "Is it OVER yet?!!."

Body aches Be sure you are comfortable at your workstation. Have a comfy seat, proper task lightening and a solid and accommodating work surface. Also, keep your most-used supplies within easy reach.

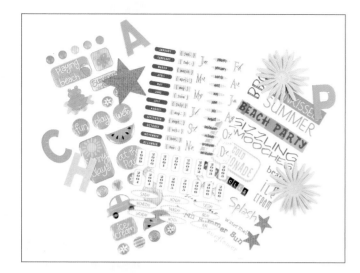

Step 5: Find Accents

Select similar accents for all the pages that you are scrapbooking within your series. Try to use accents you already own. Alter them with inks, paint, sanding, rub-ons, etc. to make them better suit your layout concept. Never underestimate the power of simple geometrics. Paper circles, squares and rectangles can be used in their native form or be spiffed up with decorative-edged scissors, glitter glue or clear gloss medium. Use only enough accents to emphasis your design.

Step 6: Design

Grab a freshly sharpened pencil, some paper and a ruler and start sketchin'. Look to magazine layouts and ads for inspiration. Can you adopt an idea for your own page? If so, think of three variations on that idea to use on your following pages.

When designing a layout, think in terms of individual page elements: photos, journaling, title and accents. Decide which element will be the focal point. Designate a place of honor for it in your page design. Arrange the rest of the elements around the focal point so that the eye moves easily across the page.

Step 7: Finalize Photos & Journaling

Now that you have a solid design plan, go back to the photos and journaling. Are you still comfortable with your earlier photo selections or do you wish to modify them? Does your layout sketch accommodate the length of your journaling? If not, perhaps you'll want to incorporate a flip-up photo. You can hide portions of your journaling underneath it. After you make these decisions, crop your photos and create your page title.

All pages by Wendy Chang

Step 8: Assemble the Pages

Collect necessary adhesives (photo sticks and tape runners for photos and journaling; glue dots for dimensional accents; foam adhesive to secure items you plan to pop up off of your background); pull out your sewing machine or needle and thread for stitched elements; collect hinges or bookbinding tape if you plan to create flip-ups or fold-outs. Tape your sketches to the wall in front of your work surface and begin assembling your layouts. Mount the photos and then the journaling block. Add the title and finish with the accents.

Instant Scrapbook Pages Using Kits

Ever since Betty Crocker introduced America to her fantastically simple and fantastically tasty cake mixes, we have counted on prepackaged products to make our lives easier. With the right combination of ingredients and some instruction, it is possible to make a perfect cake every time. With prepackaged scrapbooking kits it is possible to make perfect scrapbook pages that take the cake every time! Add some special touches to make it your own.

Carol Vaughn

Bill

A digital scrapbooking kit provides this artist with everything except the photos needed to create this great heritage page. The paper, tag, frame, buttons, fiber, paper clip and embellishment are all digital. The page is part of a heritage scrapbook the artist is creating as a gift for her mother-in-law.

Digital Downloads

When dropping by your local scrapbook or craft store is impossible, let your fingers do the walking by logging on to one of more than 100 digital scrapbook sites. There, you can purchase digital papers, embellishments and journaling treatments. Simply purchase, download and create your own digital designs OR print the supplies on photo-quality paper, cut out and go nuts!

Tristann Graves

Make the Digital Distinctive

Go from drag-and-drop to pizazz and pop!

Change the size Some of your digital accents can be enlarged or reduced. Play with the size scale for maximum effect.

Change the color Some digital elements will benefit from color shifts. That pink digital chipboard alphabet for example, can be turned blue with little effort.

Apply filters See if applying a digital special effect from your image-editing software will add a little spunk to your layout.

Make it personal Add your own touch by scanning and including a piece of memorabilia or a hand-written note.

Change your printing paper Print your digital page on a different kind of paper. Experiment with transparent and translucent materials.

CottageArts Dots-A-Fun Page Pak by Michelle Shefveland

Martha Crowther

Block Busters

Take a few minutes to concept your scrapbook page before you order a kit. Kits vary dramatically. All contain papers, but some may include die cuts, stickers, embellishments, templates, fibers, ribbons, vellum or overlays. Make sure you know what you are getting with your purchase. Shop around for the best buy. There are so many kits on the market, you should never drop your money on a kit unless your jaw has dropped first.

D Is for Devilishly Easy!

With a scrapbook kit, creating a page like this is as easy as putting down the money and putting in the time. Many kits are sold with layout suggestions and templates. They most often include papers and an assortment of embellishments.

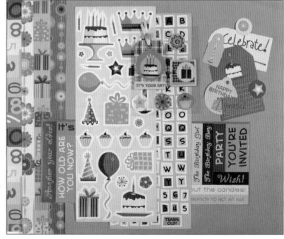

American Traditional Designs, "Celebrate" Kit

Samuel Cole

Make It Your Own

Time saved matching product can be spent gettin' creative.

Distress it Take those pristine new papers and dirty them up with brown or black stamping ink. Crumple that paper. Tear those edges. Sand, sand, sand!

Add glitter Oooh! Who doesn't love sparkle and shine? A little glitter glue will go a long way.

Paint it Want that shabby chic look? Add a bit of paint to the edges of your page.

Get dimensional Pull out the foam adhesive and start making things pop off the page.

Emboss it Add a bit of the "WOW" factor with a shiny embossed stamp.

Bang for Your Buck

This popular page kit came complete with bells and whistles. OK, no bells, no whistles, BUT it did have brads, ribbons and stickers! The artist added a few bits and pieces that he had in his own scrapbook supply box to finish the girly treasure.

Backgrounds for the Busy Body

A customized ANYTHING is built to suit our needs like a retainer fits our teeth (best example we could come up with on the fly. Forgive us.) It is our best-laid plans come to fruition. This is certainly the case when it comes to creating customized backgrounds for your scrapbook pages. While customizing a background may sound intimidating, it is actually fun to try and allows you to flex your creative muscle. Just look at these ideas and apply them to your own scrapbooking.

Print a Photo Background

Creating customized backgrounds just doesn't get any easier or more dramatic than this! Just use a stunning enlarged photo as the focal point and background for your page. Try printing the photo onto textured cardstock or fabric for a subtle and super effect.

Marla Kress

Note to self:
Use up leftovers in fridge. Make casserole. Don't worry that kids might not eat. They won't starve. Look for ways to use up leftover scrapbook supplies as well.

More Quick and Easy Backgrounds

There are gobs of ways to create customized scrapbook page backgrounds. Take a look at these!

- Color and pattern blocking
- Layers of torn papers
- Quilted paper or fabric squares
- Geometric shapes cut from coordinating papers
- Strips of patterned paper
- Collage of stickers and rub-ons
- Embossed paper that is lightly sanded
- Images cut from patterned paper, such as flowers, and adhered with foam adhesive

Erikia Ghumm

Block Buster

Feeling utterly uncreative? CLEAN! (Oh, joy!) Cleaning your workspace can help uncluttter your mind, making room for creative thoughts. As you sift through your stash, submerged ideas will rise to the surface.

Use Leftover Supplies

When you want to get funky fresh, challenge yourself to create a background with leftover supplies. Do you have enough complementary patterns to create a layered look? What about die cuts? Do you have a stash of die-cut tags or letters that can be used to build a background? Sift through your stickers to see what possibilities materialize. This artist used bits of leftover stickers and rub-ons and created a background with paper and an unused photo transfer from a previous art project.

Accents in a Flash

Think of accents like outfit accessories: The right ones will make the page while the wrong ones can be responsible for an ensemble that bombs. Good accessorizing supports the page theme without upstaging it. Look for accents in colors that add spark and textures that beg to be seen and touched. Remember not to get too fussy. Less is more.

A fantastic **stitched border** adds a hint of texture. Use a sewing machine for super swiftness.

Beguiled with **buttons**. This simple button border adds texture, shine and color. The uniqueness of the individual buttons captivates.

Erikia Ghumm

"Fast and easy" really doesn't get any faster or easier than **stamping** a delectable border. This large-motif stamp covers enough territory to accent without overpowering.

A simple length of **ribbon** adds frills in a flash. Think of ribbon to finish a photo mat, create a page border or dress up a journaling block.

Dress It Up!

There are quick and easy ways to gussy-up stickers...or die cuts...or tags...or ANY paper accent! Add cool designs with rub-ons. Add a little grunge with brown ink. Add glitz with glitter. Add age by sanding. Add some pen work.

From Trash to Treasure

Your scrapbook page is finished, but don't rush to clean up your leftover supplies! Perhaps there's a home accent just waiting to be created. This adorable wall accent materialized from the bits and pieces left over from the page on the left. The artist simply cut a circle from the orange paper, added the buttons, lettering and ribbon.

Erikia Ghumm

More Fast and Easy Accent Ideas

In nothing flat you can accent your scrapbook page and other projects. Take a look at these ideas.

Beaded accents Add clear beads to stickers and die cuts for cool looks.

Mini collages Grab an old playing card or cut a small square of paper and get artsy with leftover stickers and paper scraps.

Photo accents Unused photos, double prints and even scraps from cropped photos can be fashioned into charms, borders or photo vignettes.

Abstract designs Put your eyelets and brads to use by setting them so they spiral and bounce across your page background. Use a pen to add doodle details to frames and journaling blocks.

Mesh pocket Great for adding industrial or masculine texture to a layout, a block of mesh can be stapled to a page to hold all sorts of treasures.

Lace Just like ribbon, lace can add delicate, sophisticated or even vampish texture to your page.

Timesaving Titles

Titles may be the last element you add to your scrapbook page, but they are one of the most important. Keep titles creatively simple by using products at your immediate disposal. Taking a quick gander through your supply stash is much more efficient than taking a trip to the store (and cheaper, too!). When you find suitable letter accents and fonts, think of simple ways to dress them up.

Computer Fonts and Stickers

A simple mix of a script font and playful letter stickers creates a title with sass and ease. Reverse-print the font onto your desired paper and carefully trim with a craft knife. (Hint: The bigger and blockier the font, the easier it is to cut out.) Adhere the letters to your page and add stickers. This artist had a little extra balsa wood from a previous project, which she cut into small blocks to use as a fun background for the letter stickers. The lightweight wood adds a bit of dimension.

Heidi Schueller

Die Cuts and Chipboard

Who wants to use a boring die-cut letter when all sorts of new lettering accents exist? You do! Mix older products with new ones for fresh looks.

Rub-ons and Letter Beads

Oh, fun! Rub-ons are all the rage and are available in gazillions of styles! Letter beads are perfect for adding a whimsical touch.

Letter Stamps and Lettering Template

Reacquaint yourself with your lettering templates—they transform your handwriting into the funkiest of fonts. Mix with oversized letter stamps for a look that demands attention.

Michelle Smith

Mix Media and Styles

This funky title bounces down the right side of the page. The mix of colors, lettering styles and the vertical orientation of the title keep the eye invested. The artist used stamps, stickers, fonts and pen work to create this funky bunch.

Honey,
The kids say the puppy is getting too big to pick up. They want to get a CAT! Jamie has started preparing her doll clothes and baby buggie for a new kitty. Please talk to her!!!
John

Tips for Tempting Titles

These tricks will have you creating titles that bellow.

Mix cases Throw convention out the window and mix capital and lowercase letters for spunk.

Turn letters backward or upside down A letter that faces the wrong way will bring the right smile to your reader's face.

Stack two treatments of the same title Double your pleasure with this title trick. Be sure to pick two distinctive lettering styles for maximum impact.

Use foam adhesive for dimension How high can it go? You decide. Allow letters to tower atop each other.

Use images instead of letters An "eye" for an "i," and a "u" for a "you." Get it? Good!

Mix media We've already told you this a few times—mixing media, such as chipboard and stamps or stamps and die cuts or die cuts and chipboard is definitely a good thing.

Consider placement Titles don't always have to be placed at the top of a page. Nor do titles need to follow a straight line. Experiment by running them along the page bottom or along a diagonal and in curving lines or off-kilter designs.

Highlight letters within a word Throw a frame around a special letter or print it in a different font, color, etc.

"Scrapbook Time" = "Family Time"

This efficient use of time doubles your personal reward

Busy, busy crafters often have an "either/or" mentality when it comes to scheduling their time: I can either scrapbook OR spend time with my family. If you are one of these "this or that" folks, it is time to explore the joys of scrapbooking with your family! Family scrapbooking can be as simple as asking your children to snap a few pictures, or as complex as organizing a family scrapbooking night. Any creative and fun project that involves all the members of your family will tighten the knots that knit you together.

Stay Connected With Journaling

Do you know what the members of your family love the most about family life? Ask them! Each will have a unique favorite to share. On this page, the artist uses quotes from each family member detailing his and her favorites. This journaling technique is fun to repeat every few years to see how viewpoints and vocabularies change.

Diana Hudson

More "Favorite" Topics for Your Family to Write About

Lists of "favorites" are a wonderful way to compare and contrast personalities and opinions of family members. Ask them to write about the following:

- Favorite family trips and why
- Favorite holiday traditions, gifts, outfits
- Favorite jokes or stories
- Favorite books and movies

- Favorite pastimes or hobbies
- Favorite foods and why
- Favorite outfit they have ever owned
- Favorite family outings

Heidi Schueller

Photo Blocks

This fun home-dec project involved each member of the artist's family and was created as Christmas gifts for family members. Dad cut the wooden blocks. Mom trimmed the photos to fit the blocks. Daughters picked the photos, helped Mom adhere the trimmed photo pieces to the blocks and then helped Mom paint the boxes ("Messy, but fun!" says the artist). Mom also had daughterly assistance in picking the accents, and daughters proudly handed out the gifts at Christmas.

Getting the Family Portrait

Getting your family together for a family portrait can be a lot of work, but it is a labor of love. Here are a few tips to make the photo shoot pass most smoothly.

Feed everyone Make sure all members of the family have been fed and are well-rested. It will lessen crankiness.

Get formal and casual Start light. Snap a few "warm up" shots by allowing your family to relax and be goofy.

Be ready Have everything set up ahead of time to avoid delays that will be filled with complaints.

Use a self-timer A self-timer and/or cable release are necessary if you are going to get the entire family in the photo (unless you enlist the help of a good friend to press the button).

Find a natural and familiar setting Use a backdrop of large trees, an old building or a wraparound porch for a background that shows character and uses natural light.

Arrange the group Think shapes (visual triangle with faces, keep faces close and compensate for height) and relationships when arranging people. Look for steps and benches for posing. Ensure people are touching.

Request a specific wardrobe Go for consistent clothing (white T-shirts/jeans for casual or all black for formal). Choose two or three colors for family members and avoid busy patterns and logos. Also, long sleeves tend to be more flattering.

Record Gratitude

What better way to celebrate the holidays than with family scrapbook evenings? This Thanksgiving mini tag album records the thanks of each family member. Because of its smaller size and the repeated page design (using the same papers, embellishments and fibers on each tag), it is an easy project to complete. Prompt family members with questions, such as, "What are you thankful for?" or "What is your favorite part/meal/memory of the holiday?" Pass your camera off so that photos reflect everyone's perspective.

Cathy Shellenberg

Great Topics for Family Scrapbook Pages

Looking for inspiration for your scrapbook themes? Here you go!

- A day in the life
- Your religion
- Values and ethics
- Lessons learned
- Traditions
- Common grounds
- Physical characteristics
- The home

- Things my (parent/child/grandparent/etc.) taught me
- Family sayings
- How I'm like my (parent/grandparent/sibling/etc.)
- Growing independence
- Favorite pastimes
- School

- Family tree
- How to handle adversity
- The good, the bad, the ugly
- Holiday retrospective
- Then and now, with present immediate family as well as ancestors (fashion, traits, homes, occupations, cars)

Kathy Fesmire

Collect Recipes

Say the word "family" and chances are that images of shared mealtimes leap into your mind. It is food that brings us together. We pause during our full days to congregate around a dinner table. There, we share more than the meal itself. We share time, stories and opinions. Often, the kitchen is the best venue to ferret out all the family gossip. Because food plays such an important role in our lives, it is the perfect subject for a family scrapbook. This recipe book is a collection of the artist's favorite family recipes. She designed a recipe card on her computer, printed copies and distributed them at a family reunion. She now has a compilation of her most loved dishes. As a bonus, the recipes are all handwritten by the original family chefs.

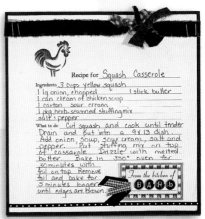

Block Buster

If you can't find the right size album for your family project then make your own! Take a long piece of paper and fold it "accordion style" (zig-zag) to the size you desire. You can bind one end by punching holes along the length and stitching it with heavy thread or string. To make a cover simply attach chip board to outside of the front and back pages. Instant album!

Scrapbook With Your Children

Some scrapbooking tasks are so easy, even a kid can do them! And that means that children can be happily productive sitting at their mini table next to your cropping table during slow-down moments. Lower your productivity expectations (just a tad!). Sticky fingerprints, wavering journaling, papers cut with corners that are far from right angles are all endearing when you think of the time and effort your child invested in the work.

Making the Background

This young artist wants the world to know what his home means to him. He constructed a paper model of his house to use as the background for his scrapbook page. Additional smaller paper house accents decorate the bottom of the page. The young artist dictated the journaling to his mother, who helped him build the scrapbook page. She added the smallest finishing touch by stitching billowing smoke from the chimney.

Kelly Goree

Let Your Kids Help

Need some safe and easy scrapbooking tasks to keep Junior occupied? Why not let him…

- punch paper shapes for backgrounds or other art.
- apply rub-ons to a frame, photo mat, background, etc.
- organize supplies: collect pens, organize by color and check tips by doodling; organize paper scraps.

- stamp a background.
- create a background with paint, ink, pens and markers (finger paint, fling paint—it can be as messy as you can handle).
- dye page elements, such as ribbon.

- crimp paper.
- distress cardboard by ripping, sanding and inking.
- ink edges.
- die cut shapes and letters.

Adding Love Notes

When Mom sat down to scrapbook this loving photo, her daughter sat down to create the journaling. She proudly wrote about how she loves her little sister. Mom dutifully helped her daughter adhere the heart-felt words to the page background with simple staples.

Creating His Own Page!

This little guy has been bitten by the scrapbooking bug! He wanted to create his own scrapbook page, so with Mom's help, he picked his own supplies, including Spiderman patterned paper. He wrote the journaling and adhered everything to the page.

Maria Burke

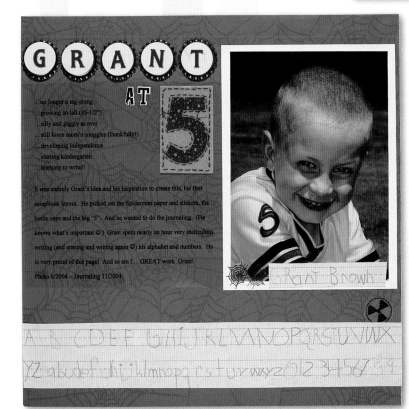

Christine Brown

On the Road Again!

Family vacations hold a treasure trove of memory opportunities. There's the excitement of planning a much-needed getaway, the inevitable mishaps, the proverbial "are we there yet?" and "Mom! Dad! I gotta GO NOW!" please. All of it culminates in hours upon hours of carefree fun. Taking your scrapbooking on the road will save you time because your memories will be captured before you even return home. The projects are also a great way to occupy idle family members during long car rides or downtime spent in the hotel.

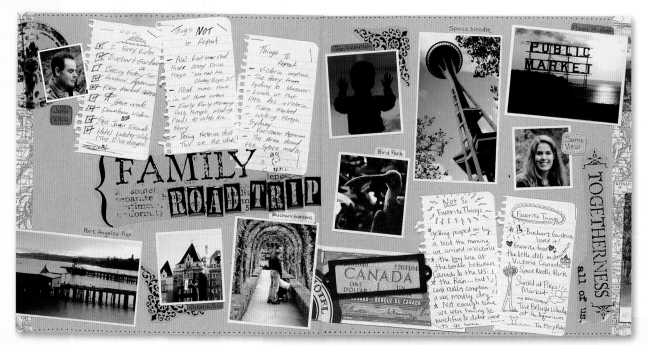

Samantha Walker

Scrapbooking Road Warrior

The key to scrapbooking on the road is no-fuss efficiency. The page above was created in the midst of a road trip. The artist kept a small notebook handy in which she journaled as the fun unfolded. She then treated the notebook pages with de-acidification spray and adhered them directly to her background. She printed her photos from a small, portable printer, which could be charged from the cigarette lighter in the car. She relied on stamping, pen details and bits of memorabilia to accent the page that captures the sense of free-footed fun.

Checklist for On-the-Road Scrapbooking

Your vacation scrapbooking bag is much more extensive than the one you might normally carry to local crops or to your child's sports practices.

- Camera with spare batteries, film (at least 1 roll per day), extra memory card, charger, cords, a disposable camera for wet or sandy situations
- Notebook to jot quick journaling notes
- Large plastic baggy to store brochures and other mementos
- Acid-free brown, black, blue pens
- Permanent and removable adhesive
- Album and page protectors
- Scissors and craft knife
- Ruler
- Colored cardstock and patterned papers complementing your destination
- Basic accents, such as eyelets and brads, mini ABC stamps, photo corners

Christine Brown

Christine Brown

The Making of a Great Vacation Scrapbook

Follow these tips when scrapbooking on the road:

- Give kids a camera (disposable or old camera).

- Use an inexpensive calendar to jot down daily details.

- Grab a newspaper when traveling to add context to journaling.

- Save mementos, such as ticket stubs, brochures, postcards, matchbooks, napkins and maps, to include in your scrapbook.

Fun Photo Cards

Post-vacation notes sent to relatives are also a fun and easy way to capture the fun. Grandma and Grandpa will be thrilled to open these cards to learn how their family spent their summer fun. They'll also be touched by the thoughtful details of the homemade treasure. The artist's sons did the journaling and picked the photos.

CHAPTER FOUR

WEBSTER'S
NEW UNIVERSAL
UNABRIDGED
DICTIONARY

2,347 pages, thumb indexed

320,000 definitions

19 encyclopedic supplements

3,000 illustrations

Full-color maps of the world

DELUXE
SECOND EDITION

I Can't Find the Right ...the Right...WORDS!

The pen is mightier than the sword, and when you pair it with a good set of sharp scissors and a craft knife, you can be an unstoppable historical preservationist! That is…if you know how to wield each of these tools to achieve the greatest results. Unfortunately, unless pinned against the wall, many scrapbookers do their best to wiggle out of having to journal on their scrapbook pages. They seem to view text as their foe instead of their friend—the vehicle that allows them to add details such as "when," "where," "who" and "why" to their scrapbook artwork. It is the written word that makes it possible for crafters to add a story line to their scrapbook pages.

No matter how lacking in courage you feel about the idea of journaling, you simply must face the need to do so head on. But here's the good news: There are many, many different ways to journal and many, many of them are so simple they're guaranteed to be painless.

Note to self:
Write Mom
Write proposal for boss
Write kid's teachers thank-you letters... (last year's teachers and this year's teachers)
Write grocery list
JOURNAL!

CLASS! Write 100 Times, "I Love to Journal"

Get over your writing hang-ups

Nobody ever said writing was easy, but then neither was mastering your multiplication tables, learning to speak publicly or parenting. The road to learning is often arduous and most of us stumble about a bit before getting our footing. And yet…the places we go when we continue to put one foot in front of the other!

We all have the knowledge we need in order to write competently. After all, those tactics were drilled into us in school. DO capitalize first letters in sentences. DON'T use double negatives. DO use three examples if you wish to make a point. DON'T have run-on sentences. But as much as those lessons benefit us when it comes to writing "correctly," the sheer number of laws left many afraid to put pen to paper because the "F" letter was always lurking in the wings.

Well, guess what? We are grown up, and it's time to take the best and leave the rest of our education as we move forward as writers. When journaling on our scrapbook pages, we can make up our own rules. The only "wrong" is not journaling at all.

Shelly Boyd

Just Put Some Words, ANY WORDS, Down on Paper

The hardest part of journaling is getting started. Most often, once the first several sentences are down on paper, the others will cooperatively follow. Many professional writers require themselves to write a certain number of words or pages each day. It doesn't matter if the words are "good" or not. What matters is that they are flowing. They can always be rewritten, discarded or expanded upon. But nothing can be done with "nothing," so forging forward is the key to success.

Diana Hudson, Photo: © Greg McCracken, iStock Photo

Block Buster

When you simply can't figure out what to put on your scrapbook page, begin with basic information: who, what, when, where and why. (Who is in the photo? What was going on? When did it take place and where? Why did it happen?)

Pen or Keypad? It's Your Choice!

No matter how proficient you are at typing, you may find that the feeling of a pen in your hand opens up the avenues to your best writing by forcing you to slow down and really contemplate the thoughts you are trying to convey. On the other hand, computers make it possible for a rush of thoughts to pour from your fingertips. And don't forget that wonderful invention called Spell Check that can turn spelling dunces into spelling wizards. Experiment to discover which method of journaling suits you best.

Going to THAT Place

Writers have a way of closing out the distractions of the "real" world and slipping into one of their own making where their best work gets done. This time is as important to them as the hours they spend at their computers. In fact novelist Lois Duncan recalls spending many of her childrens' nap times deep in her own "dream time" in a backyard lawn chair. While the neighbors may have thought her lazy, she was actually working out the next steps in the plots she was working on. Once dream time was over, she returned to the computer, ready to write the next chapter!

Jessica Sprague

Schedule Dream Time

Dreaming time usually doesn't happen without some planning. If you want to tackle a truly important journaling effort, consider the following:

- Schedule at least an hour when you will be totally alone and know that nobody will be making demands upon you.

- Turn off cell phones and step away from your computer. Set your watch to remind you when your dreaming time is up.

- Leave your office and find someplace comfortable (but not sooo comfortable that you are likely to fall asleep!).

- Take a small notebook and a pen with you to your dream place. Jot down notes so the thoughts don't slip away.

- If you are focusing on journaling about a particular subject, draw it into your mind. Visualize it. Focus on the tastes and sounds related to.

- Go with the flow of your thoughts instead of trying to regulate or control them.

- When your time is up, take a few minutes to flesh out any inspirational thoughts that came to you.

Nudge Yourself With Journaling Prompts

Where to begin? Sometimes it takes a little nudge to get our thoughts churning. Challenge yourself with a journaling prompt that is related to the photo you are planning to scrapbook. The prompt could focus on the emotions you have surrounding the page, or events that you have experienced that are either similar or very different from the one you are scrapbooking. Have a pencil in hand or be seated in front of your computer. Focus on the prompt and then let the thoughts flow.

Shannon Taylor

Kick-Start Your Journaling

These prompts may set your journaling mind in gear:

- When I look at this photo I feel…
- I can hardly believe that…
- Once upon a time things were different…
- The best thing and the worst thing about it was…
- I'll never understand…
- My own personal definition of "blessed" is…
- I owe _____ so much for teaching me…

- It was worth it because in the end…
- The colors, sounds and smells of _____ reminded me of…
- I remember, when I was a little girl, I always dreamed…
- The greatest truth of all is…
- If I knew my world were ending, I'd want to…
- The first thing I saw was…
- What I love most about _____ is….

Take the Pressure Off the Pen

Super-fast journaling ideas: Do them! (to make it short and sweet)

You may write the Great American Novel next week, but this week you've got too much on your plate to even think about it. It's time to focus on a bite-sized project like journaling for a single scrapbook page. If even THAT seems too demanding, we've got some ideas that you can crank out in less time than it takes for your kids to walk home from the bus stop.

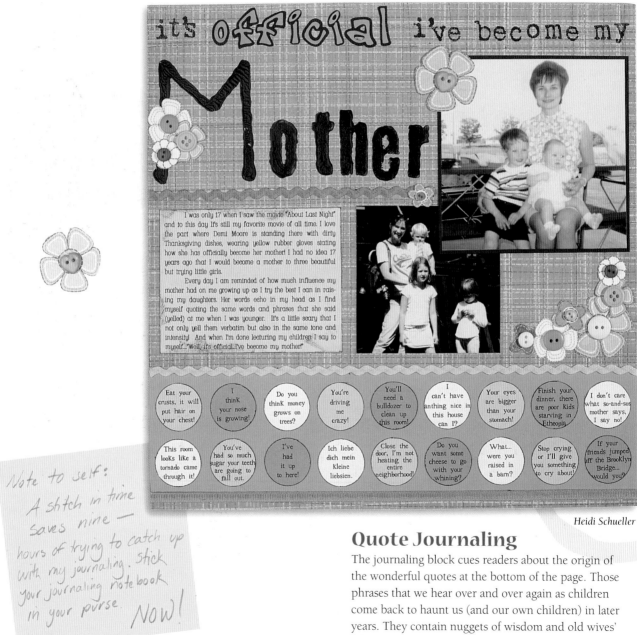

Heidi Schueller

Note to self:
A stitch in time
saves nine —
hours of trying to catch up
with my journaling. Stick
your journaling notebook
in your purse. NOW!

Quote Journaling

The journaling block cues readers about the origin of the wonderful quotes at the bottom of the page. Those phrases that we hear over and over again as children come back to haunt us (and our own children) in later years. They contain nuggets of wisdom and old wives' tales that are worth preserving.

Take a Page From Your Book

If you keep a personal journal, you are steps ahead. It can be your own personal reference tool for scrapbooking. It can even be INCLUDED in your scrapbooking. For this layout the artist photocopied a passage from her journal and used the copy as journaling on her artwork.

Erikia Ghumm

What's a Journal Ever Done for ME?

Plenty. While starting a journal can be intimidating, keeping one becomes addicting. Daily (well, almost daily. OK, weekly. Listen, we'll settle for monthly!) writing helps you process the world around you and keep track of your inspirations. Make it fun—buy a really special journal that you are drawn to and a really fantastic pen that complements your handwriting. Schedule some quiet time, sit down and write. Write whatever you want, just keep at it.

Erikia Ghumm

Write Me a Letta', The Sooner the Betta'

Remember those thank-you notes your mom insisted you write after every Christmas-present-opening extravaganza? Grasping a pencil in a reluctant hand, you scrawled a few words that were supposed to sound grateful but often came off as somewhat short of gracious (piles of toys just waiting to be explored and we were writing stupid letters!). If you'd asked us then if letter writing would ever become enjoyable, the answer would have been an absolute and immediate NO. How wrong we were! Letter writing can be fun and is even more satisfying when you use it as a form of journaling on your scrapbook pages.

Mary MacAskill

Letter Writing Journaling

Dear Reader,

You have been writing letters since you could hold a pencil. Put those letter-writing skills to use on your scrapbook pages. Just pretend that you are writing a letter to, or about, the topic you are scrapping. Do it first person, or for a bit more fun, write from the perspective of your pet or someone else.

Debbie Hodge

Kids' Notes

Let the younger generation take some of the journaling duties off of your hands by putting a pencil and piece of paper in theirs! Give your favorite little scribe a topic and ask him to tell you what's on his mind.

Block Buster

So, you're working on this scrapbook page, and your head seems to have your words in a vice grip. Breathe. Sit for a second and visualize your best friend. She is so awesome! She knows you and your idiosyncrasies, and you tell her everything. Now, pretend you are going to tell her about the memory that is unfolding on your scrapbook page. Don't leave out any of the details, and simply tell it like it is, in your own words, in your own voice.

What REALLY Smart People Have Said About Writing...

"The ideal view for daily writing, hour for hour, is the blank brick wall of a cold-storage warehouse. Failing this, a stretch of sky will do, cloudless if possible." - Edna Ferber

"Write your story as it needs to be written. Write it honestly, and tell it as best you can. I'm not sure that there are any other rules. Not ones that matter." - Neil Gaiman

"My most important piece of advice to all you would-be writers: When you write, try to leave out all the parts readers skip." - Elmore Leonard

From the Desks of the Bards

Numb-brain. It's an affliction you are unlikely to read about in the local newspaper, but one most overstretched moms can diagnose easily. Symptoms include standing in front of an ATM and forgetting your oh-too-familiar PIN, wondering whether the puppy gets two pills once a day or one pill twice a day, trying to remember how you spell the word "who" (hoo? hew?). When you are journaling and numb-brain strikes, give yourself a break. Use the words penned by some of the sharpest literary brains ever published.

Samantha Walker, Lyrics: John Phillip Sousa

Lyrics Journaling

Wanna write about love? surfing? car rides? hobbies? death? friendship? seasons? God? family? holidays? historical events? No problem! Those topics and many others have been immortalized by songwriters throughout the centuries. The lyrics make wonderful fast and easy journaling on scrapbook pages.

Block Buster

Transcribe the words to the song you wish to use on your scrapbook page. Print it on paper or on a transparency and mount it on your background paper. Or, photocopy sheet music that includes the lyrics and musical notes. Mount that directly on your page. Old sheet music is easily found at garage sales and flea markets, if you wish to use the original musical score as part of your art.

Katie Watson, Poem: Katie Watson

Kathleen Broadhurst, Poem: Emily Dickinson

Poetry Journaling

Good poetry has a way of corralling a concept and articulating it in a way that most of us cannot. The words sing and the message is astute. When you find yourself floundering to write your own verse, borrow from a bard.

Write Your Own Poetry

If you spend poetry-writing sessions playing the "rhyme chime" (I have a cat and she is—black as a bat/ all that/cool as your hat/walks pitty-pat/mean as a rat), STOP! Turn your efforts to writing unrhymed verse that more quickly and surely captures the mood of your page.

- Close your eyes and think about your theme. Let yourself smell, feel, hear and taste it. Jot down adjectives you associate with those senses and use them in your poem. Consider beginning your poem with the page title. Follow with lists of adjectives. End the poem with a phrase that sums up the page theme.

- What other places or things do you associate with those adjectives? You may want to use these as analogies or comparisons in your poetry. Example: The snowflakes on your boot toes melted like ice cream melts on a summer tongue.

- What is the underlying message of the scrapbook page you are designing? If you are writing the poem to share that message, make sure it is clear in the poem. Consider starting the poem by stating the theme. Example: I couldn't love you more if…(use the next lines of the poem for examples) and then end the poem by repeating the first line: I couldn't love you more.

The Least Words Possible
Need we say more?

Focus on a Family Member

Think of this as a loving family tell-all. Great for celebrating birthdays, accomplishments or even to help one get through a challenging time, pages such as these are easy to do. Simply pick a beloved family member and ask the other family members to contribute some kind words. In this page, the artist asked the family to wax poetic about his partner. The resulting journaling is a collection of heartfelt quotes easily printed and trimmed into captions.

Samuel Cole

Get the Masses Involved

Time to call in the reinforcements! Even if you are a prolific journaler, you may eventually run low on words. Or, you could be seeking perspectives about events that vary from your own. Family members may have memories about people, places or things before your time. For all of these reasons, and more, it is fun to use the journaling of others on your scrapbook layouts.

Circle Journal Start a journal in which you have enlisted a group of people. Tab pages throughout the journal on which you have jotted questions or events. Encourage family members to write in each section before passing the journal to the next person on the list. When the journal is returned to you, include their contributions on scrapbook pages.

Interview Set a time to meet and interview older members of your family. Make the event casual and early in the day when everyone is energized and ready to chat. A recorder is often the easiest way to get a non-stilted interview. Take notes as well (tape-recorder malfunctions really stink!). Do not ask "yes/no" questions (Example: Did you like school? Instead, ask leading questions: What did you like and dislike about school?).

Letter Writing Campaign Whether by the traditional method, or e-mail, begin writing relatives or friends and asking them to respond to certain questions or to share their ideas about topics. Include spaces in your letter for their replies. Include a self-addressed/stamped envelope to make it easy for them to return the letter.

Timeline Journaling

Events unfold so slowly that too often we fail to notice changes as they take place. Timeline journaling provides perspective by building forward from a determined date. The measure of time is the yardstick against which you can assess progress.

Kelli Dickinson

Bullet Journaling

Forget complete sentences, if you wish, and stop worrying about either paragraphs or continuity. Just get those facts and ideas down as fast as possible using bullet journaling!

Kay Rogers

Prefab Journaling

Manufacturers of modern scrapbooking supplies make scrapbooking almost effortless with roll-on adhesives, precut frames and mats and coordinating packaged papers. They also rescue reluctant journalers with preprinted transparencies, papers and embellishments that convey a huge number of messages. Shop around for the perfect prefab products to help you in your journaling endeavors.

Martha Crowther

Block Buster

Transparencies can be tricky to adhere. Try…

- Clear-drying spray adhesive
- Brads
- Eyelets
- Staples
- Hiding adhesive marks with other page elements

Transparencies Do the Trick

Transparencies are words or phrases printed on transparent polyester film. They are sold singly or are grouped by theme in packages. You may create your own by printing your thoughts on a plain transparency. (Available at any office-supply store—set your printer to "transparency setting" and print on the "rough" side of the sheet.) Vary the font styles to make them more interesting. Layer the transparency on top of photos.

Prefab Journaling Finds

If you don't wish to purchase prefab journaled products, keep your eyes open for other printed materials that may be used to supply information on your scrapbook pages.

- Programs and brochures
- Restaurant napkins, coasters, disposable menus
- Newspaper and newsletter clippings
- Brochures, maps
- Internet printouts of locations or events
- Copies of marriage licenses, drivers licenses, graduation announcements, diplomas, work reviews

Stickers and Such

Stickers are available with a multitude of words and sayings. They also come in a large range of colors, sizes, shapes and textures. How much easier can journaling be than simply peeling off the backing of a sticker and applying it to your scrapbook page? Combine a variety of stickers to flesh out your journaling message.

Wendy Chang

Maria Burke

Outside

This page may be all about the outside, but it is inside your local scrapbook or hobby store that you'll have the fun of selecting papers that are printed with journaling! The right paper can convey in color, words and typography the exact mood you wish to project on your scrapbook page. Add a small personalized journaling block if you wish, or simply finish the layout with a spunky title.

Hidden Journaling

Peekaboo! I see you! Or, maybe hide-and-seek. Hidden journaling elements promote fun and games on any scrapbook page because they entice the reader to explore the page. But, they also have a practical side. Hidden journaling expands a scrapbook page. By containing the journaling on the back or inside of an element, you, dear and efficient scrapbooker, are maximizing your layout space. You now have more room for those amazing photos! This technique also is a discreet way to package journaling of a personal nature.

Block Buster

Easy ways to hide journaling

- Envelopes
- Pull tags
- Photos that fold open or flip up
- Lightweight mini journals attached to a page

Nic Howard

Tucked Away

Sometimes you want to shout your story to the world. Other times, you simply want to share it only with those willing to really listen. If your scrapbook page falls under the latter category, consider tucking personal journaling behind a photo, just as this artist did. The page shows a carefree child running happily on the beach, while the journaling details his daily struggles and the immense love his family has for him. To re-create, print journaling on cardstock and mat. Slip under an unadhered edge of a photo.

Open Sesame!

Hinges and little tabs demanding that you "PULL!" They are great indicators that hidden treasure lies on a scrapbook page. Hinges are easy mechanisms for creating flip-open journaling elements. You can purchase fancy hinges at your neighborhood scrapbook or craft store, or head to the linen closet or garage to rustle some up. If hinges seem a little too "tool time" for you, try using book-binding tape.

Wendy Chang

An independent spirit, Aidan insists on trying everything on her own. She'll watch you carefully. She'll watch you often. But at the end of the day, by design, she'll pick it up, and figure it out herself. At the beach in May, she wanted to fly the kite. And so, she just picked it up, studied it a bit, and off she ran, trailing the flowing colors behind her. As happy as can be, it did not matter that the kite was not technically in the air. All that mattered was that she was doing it, her way. She was so free! As parents, we watch, and encourage her. Her sense of determination and independence will be an incredible asset as an adult. And so when that independence manifests in stubborn misbehavior, we keep the big goal in mind, and do our best to guide her around that fine line between independence, and obnoxious self centeredness. We will be the first to admit that it is a challenge. But such a worthy one. Topanga Beach, California. 2006.

Note to self:

Hide a card for John under his pillow. Remind him that I love him, even though I often keep my thoughts hidden. Make a commitment to open up and talk about feelings more often.

It's Already Written, So Use It!

Life is so complicated that most of us navigate our way through the days by leap-frogging from one stay-on-task notation to the next. Once the events or obligations are through, we toss away the reminders and turn our minds forward to the next set of tasks. Stop! Those reminders of daily activities can serve as wonderful journaling on pages. They reflect the day-to-day rather than momentous life events, which make them a true documentary of our times.

Linda Garrity

Beach Day!

Count down to the big day! Whether you are looking forward to a wedding, a vacation or the beginning of a new school year, you are probably using a calendar to line up preparations. Once the event has passed, either photocopy entries related to the event, or cut the calendar into pieces. Mount the calendar entries on your art when scrapbooking the occasion.

Note to self
SCRAPBOOK!

Count blessings everyday,
kids may keep me on
my toes picking up and
cleaning and cooking
but the physical
activity keeps
me thin-ish.

FETCH!

loyal

Note to self:
Remember to breath
when puppy takes the
steak off the grill. At
least he no longer chews
scrap book supplies!

I ♥ My
DOG

Don't forget a
little "ME" time
every day...

ELO

Martha Crowther

Stick With It!

Sticky notes can pile up and most often we sweep the growing towers into that
week's trash bag without hesitation. But what easier way to journal on your
scrapbook page than to do so with sticky notes? Use several dozen to create
background paper, or scatter them around for a casual reading experience. When
journaling is this easy, you are sure to stick to it.

Never-fail Templates

Use these terrific layout templates when you need a fresh idea for a scrapbook layout. You may wish to reproduce a template exactly, or modify it to better showcase your elements. The templates range from symmetrical (#3) to less structured (#8).

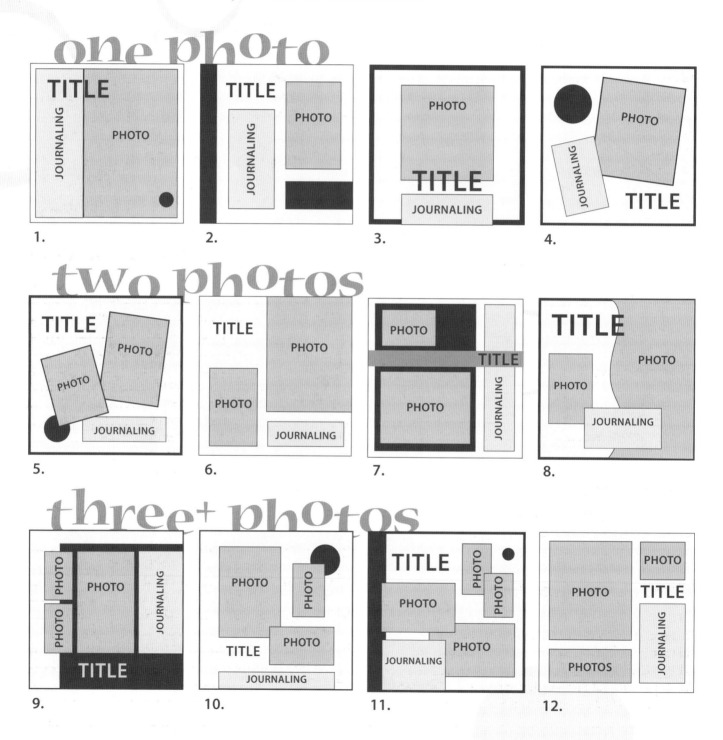

Get Ready! Get Set! Go...Shopping! *(copy this page for an instant shopping list)*

Organizational Items

- ❏ Photo boxes/envelopes, ❏ Negative sleeves
- ❏ Memorabilia keepers
- Albums ❏ 6 x 6" ❏ 8 x 8" ❏ 12 x 12" ❏ 8½ x 11" ❏ specialty
- ❏ Filler pages, Size_____
- ❏ Page protectors, Size_____

Paper

Cardstock/s
- ❏ Red, ❏ Orange, ❏ Yellow, ❏ Brown, ❏ Green, ❏ Blue,
- ❏ Purple, ❏ Pink, ❏ Black, ❏ White,
- ❏ Other _____
- ❏ Patterned paper, Colors/s_____

  Themes_____

- ❏ Vellum, Color/s _____

  Pattern/s_____

- ❏ Specialty paper_____

  Color/s_____

  Type/themes_____

Adhesives

- ❏ Photo splits, ❏ Double-sided tape, ❏ Tape runner,
- ❏ Glue pen, ❏ Glue stick, ❏ Embellishment glue
- ❏ Foam adhesive

Tools and Supplies

- ❏ Small scissors, ❏ Regular scissors, ❏ Large scissors
- ❏ Specialty scissors (i.e. dedicated fabric shears)
- ❏ Craft knife, ❏ Craft knife blades, ❏ Paper trimmer
- ❏ Punches (type/s) _____
- ❏ Circle cutter, ❏ Self-healing cutting mat, ❏ Sandpaper,
- ❏ Bone Folder, ❏ Eyelet-setting tools, ❏ Tweezers,
- ❏ Other_____

Writing Tools

- ❏ Pen (nib width)_____ (color)_____
- ❏ Pen (nib width)_____ (color)_____
- ❏ Pen (nib width)_____ (color)_____

- ❏ Marker (width)_____ (color)_____
- ❏ Marker (width)_____ (color)_____
- ❏ Marker (width)_____ (color)_____

Rulers and Templates

- ❏ Cork-backed metal ruler, ❏ Lettering templates,
- ❏ Shape template, ❏ Other_____

Stamps, Stickers and Die Cuts

- ❏ Stamp (design/s) _____ (size/s)_____
- ❏ Stamp (design/s) _____ (size/s)_____
- ❏ Stamp (design/s) _____ (size/s)_____
- ❏ Ink _____ (color)_____
- ❏ Ink _____ (color)_____
- ❏ Ink _____ (color)_____
- ❏ Sticker/s _____ (theme)_____
- ❏ Sticker/s _____ (theme)_____
- ❏ Sticker/s _____ (theme)_____
- ❏ Die cut/s _____ (theme)_____
- ❏ Die cut/s _____ (theme)_____
- ❏ Die cut/s _____ (theme)_____

Embellishments

- ❏ Eyelets (color/s)_____ (size/s)_____
- ❏ Brads (color/s)_____ (size/s)_____
- ❏ Fibers (type)_____ (color/s)_____
  (amount)_____
- ❏ Ribbon_____ (color/s)_____
  (amount)_____
- ❏ Bookplate (size/s)_____ (color/s)_____
  (style/s)_____
- ❏ Frame/s (size/s)_____ (color/s)_____
  (style/s)_____
- ❏ Other_____

Index

$14.95
Can. $19.95

Scrapbooking for the TIME IMPAIRED

Oh yes, you DO have time to scrapbook!!!

It's true that you have meals to make, a family to take care of, a career to pursue, a dog to walk, and exercise classes to attend. And while those activities keep you running, they're part of the busy and rewarding life you'll want to celebrate on terrific quick and easy scrapbook pages. This ingenious and entertaining guide shows you how.

- Open your eyes to layout and design possibilities as you drive carpools or cheer on your soccer champs.

- Take advantage of time management ideas and ways to get around the dreaded "writer's block."

- Out of supplies? No worries. Raid your own junk drawer, closet, and home office for everything from wrapping paper to yarn, and then use them in your layouts.

- Explore the way technology can be an overloaded person's best friend.

- And that's just a small sample of what you'll find inside!

Complete with Never-Fail Templates and dozens of great layouts, *Scrapbooking for the Time Impaired* will make this creative pastime a can-do (and Must-Do) part of your hectic and wonderful life.

Kerry Arquette and Andrea Zocchi have authored and created a line of popular scrapbooking books, including *The Joy of Scrapbooking*, *Scrapbooking Sports*, *The Scrapbooker's Color Palette*, and a number of books for Kodak Books. They both live with families in Denver, Colorado.

ISBN-13: 978-1-60059-003-0
ISBN-10: 1-60059-003-9

9 781600 590030   51495

LARK BOOKS

A Division of
Sterling Publishing
New York

$14.95
Can. $19.95

Scrapbooking
for the TIME IMPAIRED

Oh yes, you DO have time to scrapbook!!!

It's true that you have meals to make, a family to take care of, a career to pursue, a dog to walk, and exercise classes to attend. And while those activities keep you running, they're part of the busy and rewarding life you'll want to celebrate on terrific quick and easy scrapbook pages. This ingenious and entertaining guide shows you how.

- Open your eyes to layout and design possibilities as you drive carpools or cheer on your soccer champs.

- Take advantage of time management ideas and ways to get around the dreaded "writer's block."

- Out of supplies? No worries. Raid your own junk drawer, closet, and home office for everything from wrapping paper to yarn, and then use them in your layouts.

- Explore the way technology can be an overloaded person's best friend.

- And that's just a small sample of what you'll find inside!

Complete with Never-Fail Templates and dozens of great layouts, *Scrapbooking for the Time Impaired* will make this creative pastime a can-do (and Must-Do) part of your hectic and wonderful life.

Kerry Arquette and Andrea Zocchi have authored and created a line of popular scrapbooking books, including *The Joy of Scrapbooking*, *Scrapbooking Sports*, *The Scrapbooker's Color Palette*, and a number of books for Kodak Books. They both live with their families in Denver, Colorado.

ISBN-13: 978-1-60059-003-0
ISBN-10: 1-60059-003-9

51495

9 781600 590030

LARK BOOKS

A Division of
Sterling Publishing
New York